a CHEF in every HOME

the complete family cookbook

Culinary Regards.

KUNAL KAPUR

Kunal
11/2/2014.

RANDOM HOUSE INDIA

Published by Random House India in 2014
1
Copyright © Kunal Kapur 2014

Random House Publishers India Private Limited
Windsor IT Park, 7th Floor
Tower-B, A-1, Sector-125
Noida 201301, UP

Random House Group Limited
20 Vauxhall Bridge Road
London SW1V 2SA
United Kingdom

978 81 8400 3529

This book is sold subject to the condition that it shall not, by way of trade or otherwise, be lent, resold, hired out, or otherwise circulated without the publisher's prior consent in any form of binding or cover other than that in which it is published and without a similar condition including this condition being imposed on the subsequent purchaser.

Book design: Anjora Noronha
Photography © Shirish Sen
Front cover image © Md Sabi
Printed and bound in India by Replika Press Private Limited

For my Mummy and Papa

Caramel Bananas (pg 148)

Contents

Introduction 6

Cooking and Kitchen Basics 9

Weights and Measurements 12

17 *Smacky Starters*

43 *The Essentials: Condiments, Dips, Relishes, Chutneys*

55 *Healthy and Fun Menus for Kids*

75 *Salads and Soups for the Soul*

85 *Breads and Rice*

97 *Hearty Main Courses*

129 *Sweet Tooth: Desserts*

List of Recipes 150

Acknowledgements 154

A Note on the Author 156

A Note on the Food Stylist 157

A Note on the Photographer 157

A Note on the Food Researcher 157

Introduction

My journey with food began in my roaring old kitchen at home. In those days, the size of a kitchen was usually bigger than a living room; it was the one area where space was never compromised. I was raised in a joint family, which meant that there were many mouths to feed. Back then cooking was a ritual more than a daily chore. My oldest memories are of me sitting on an upturned empty oil canister placed on top of our kitchen counter watching my father, uncles, and my grandfather cook. Unlike most Indian households, all the men in my big, rambling family loved to cook.

My father would cook almost every Sunday and I would be given the task of Chief Stirrer. The big advantage of being Chief Stirrer was that my father would teach me the names of the ingredients that went into whatever I was stirring. I am sure he did that only to sharpen my vocabulary but what he also managed to do was teach me a glossary of ingredients that would one day become my life and my very reason of existence. I owe everything to the kitchen and people of my house for inculcating in me the love of cooking and the joy of sharing and eating.

Being a chef for twelve years did a lot to boost the clichéd ego in me. Emboldened by my culinary school degree and my success after it, the memories of my childhood and our kitchen, where some of the tastiest meals came from, began to fade. I now only spoke culinary jargon—technically correct dishes and recipes—but when the moment of truth came, I was left speechless. It was at the auditions for *MasterChef India* (2010), when I saw thousands of home cooks line up with amazing home-cooked food, that made me realize something important: Good food can come from anyone. After four seasons of *MasterChef India*, travelling across the country, hunting for talent, seeking out good food, I stumbled on a truth that there is A Chef in Every Home.

From choosing to be a chef at a time when it was considered a job for the hopeless to being awarded the Sir Edmund Hillary Fellowship in the field of Food and Beverage by the prime minister of New Zealand, it has been a long journey filled with mistakes, learning, creation, joy, travel, exploration and understanding food, people, and cultures at a totally different level. And I wanted nothing more than to share these experiences as recipes in the form of a book.

Food is a form of expression and *A Chef in Every Home* will help bring out the chef in you. All you need is a guide, a mentor to get started. I decided to write a book to help you through your own food journey, through your kitchen firsts and your kitchen disasters. All the recipes that I've outlined have been put together in the easiest way possible, so that not only do you get a great dish at the end, you also have fun making it. The recipes are designed to break the myth that some dishes are considered 'aspirational' or 'gourmet', or in other words 'difficult'. Many of the recipes allow room to innovate and include ingredients of your choice, which will build and boost your confidence and establish the fact that before anything else cooking is fun, doable, and very addictive.

Using simple ingredients from your kitchen you can make world cuisine, and thoroughly impress your friends and family while you're at it! This book brings to the table a range of complete meals from starters, soups, main courses, rice and breads, accompaniments, relishes, and desserts. I've kept it simple so that you can cook all this and more using mostly the ingredients in your kitchen.

So what are you waiting for? Grab the book and let's cook!

Cooking and Kitchen Basics

Not all kitchens are equipped in the same way. In order to use this book to the fullest, you should stock your kitchen with certain cooking equipment and also understand a few basic cooking techniques and weights and measurements. I put them together in the most simplified manner for you.

Cooking Equipment

Pots and Pans

Make sure that you have a good mix of heavy and light weight pots and pans in your kitchen.

Lighter pans are good for boiling and stir frying, whereas heavy pots and pans are better for slow cooking.

Use the appropriate pot or a pan as per the requirement of the dish. It is better to have a mix of aluminum, cast iron, and stainless steel pots and pans at home.

Knives

You require a simple chef's knife, peeler, and a palette knife to try out all the recipes.

A study suggests that more fingers are cut while using a blunt knife rather than a sharp knife. Sharpen your knives periodically.

Remember to always wash and dry your knives after use.

Try and keep all knives separately in a wooden block.

If you are not confident of handling a 7" to 9" SS blade, switch to a smaller knife but make sure that it has a good grip and a stainless steel blade.

Food Processing Machines

This book uses recipes that require an oven. For best results, use a convection oven.

Electric whisks, blenders, graters, mini choppers, juicers, and food processors make cooking more convenient.

Ensure that you always buy branded electrical equipment for your kitchen.

Ensure that you read and follow the safety instructions listed on the equipment.

Always clean and dry the all equipment before and after use.

Baking Cutters, Moulds, Trays

Stock your kitchen with stainless steel fancy cutters that come in various shapes and sizes.

Different moulds for cupcakes, pies, and cold desserts help in creating attractive shapes. You can use aluminum moulds, silicon moulds, or non stick moulds for ease of cooking.

Choose the baking trays wisely. Check that your baking trays fit your oven at home. Light aluminum or non stick trays or even silicon mats do a great job.

Cooking Techniques

Blanching is flash cooking of vegetables or fruits in boiling water and then immersing them immediately in cold water. This is usually done to easily peel the skin off. Blanching of bones refers to a quick boil of bones and then washing the bones under cold. This process cleans the bones of impurities making the stock clean and clear.

Breading is the process of applying breadcrumbs to certain foods to get a crispy and crunchy texture. For example, you will use this technique in the Pea and Potato Croquette and Fried Mozzarella Sticks recipes.

Searing is a technique in which meat is put on a hot pan to get a nice brown colour on the outside. This action seals in the juices of the meat. Once meat is seared, it is usually cooked in an oven at a low temperature so that it cooks from the inside.

Folding is to gently mix using light lifting actions of two or more ingredients of different density. The best example is when flour is folded into whipped eggs—it is gently folded so that the air from the whisked eggs does not escape.

Sautéing means to fry food quickly in a hot pan, stirring it from time to time. It is a French word which means jump or bounce.

Whisking is a process of blending/mixing ingredients in such a way so as to incorporate air into them to make them light in texture. For example, whisking egg whites to make them frothy. Whisking is also used in mixing batters or curries or to get rid of lumps.

Poaching is a technique of cooking food submerged in a liquid on very gentle heat. The liquid can be any stock—wine, juice, or milk.

Basting is a method of applying or brushing any liquid on a food to enhance its flavour, colour, or to seal in moisture.

Weights and Measurements

1 tablespoon (tbsp)	3 teaspoons (tsp)
1/4 cup	4 tablespoons
1/3 cup	5 tablespoons + 1 teaspoon
1/2 cup	8 tablespoons
2/3 cup	10 tablespoons + 2 teaspoons
3/4 cup	12 tablespoons
1 cup	48 teaspoons
1 cup	16 tablespoons
8 fluid ounces (fl oz)	1 cup
1 pint (pt)	2 cups
1 quart (qt)	2 pints
4 cups	1 quart
1 gallon (gal)	4 quarts
16 ounces (oz)	1 pound (lb)

US to Metric

Capacity	Weight
1 teaspoon	5 ml
1 tablespoon	15 ml
1 fluid oz	30 ml
1/5 cup	47 ml
1 cup	237 ml
2 cups (1 pint)	473 ml
4 cups (1 quart)	.95 litre
4 quarts (1 gal)	3.8 litres

Metric to US

Capacity	Weight
1 millilitre	1/5 teaspoon
5 ml	1 teaspoon
15 ml	1 tablespoon
100 ml	3.4 fluid oz
240 ml	1 cup
1 litre	34 fluid oz
	4.2 cups
	2.1 pints
	1.06 quarts
	0.26 gallon

Cups	Grams
1.0	236.58824
3/4	177.44118
1/2	118.29412
1/4	59.14706
1/3	78.86274

Stocks

Stocks are an essential part of cooking. They are a favoured liquid base for making curries, soups, stews. It is made by the prolonged simmering of bones, herbs, vegetable and spices. A good stock can make your dish a star, and vice versa unfortunately. Here I will teach you how to make both a vegetarian and non-vegetarian stock.

Chicken Stock and Mutton Stock

Preparation time **10 mins**
Cooking time **1 ½ hrs**

1 kg chicken bones
3 litres water
1 cup onion, diced
1 cup carrots, diced

4 garlic cloves, smashed
1 ginger knob, smashed
5 peppercorns, crushed
1 bay leaf

In a deep vessel, add chicken bones and sufficient water to cover.

Give it a quick boil and immediately strain. Discard the water and wash the bones.

Place the bones in a clean pan with 3 litres water and bring to a boil and then allow it to simmer. Add onion, carrots, garlic, ginger, bay leaf, and peppercorns.

Simmer for 1 hour 15 minutes uncovered. Then strain through a fine mesh or a muslin cloth. Cool and refrigerate.

Vegetable Stock*

Preparation time 10 mins
Cooking time 1 hr

2 litres water
1 cup vegetable trimmings**
1 cup turnip, diced
1 cup onion, diced
2 cup carrots, diced

4 garlic cloves, smashed
1 ginger knob, smashed
5 peppercorns, crushed
1 bay leaf

Wash all the vegetables thoroughly in running water. In a deep vessel, add 2 litres water and all the vegetables, bay leaf, and peppercorns.

Give it a boil and allow it to simmer for an hour. Strain through a fine mesh or a muslin cloth and use as desired.

*This recipe of vegetable stock can be used in the preparations specifically listed in the recipes in this book.

**Vegetable trimmings should preferably be of root vegetables or unused stalks of cauliflower or broccoli.

Smacky Starters

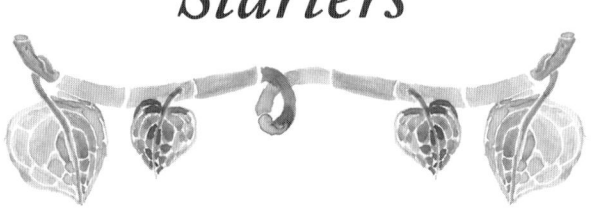

Preparation time 20 mins
Cooking time 10 mins

Raw Papaya Kebabs with Mango Salsa Serves 2

I was never fond of papayas and my first time cooking raw papaya happened a decade ago—a friend of mine made me taste a raw papaya chutney which left me stumped. Much to my surprise, the chutney was tasty but the most interesting thing was that it had a good bite to it, which chutneys generally don't have. And thus my perspective on the humble papaya changed forever.

2 cups raw papaya, thickly grated
1 cup raw potato, thickly grated
1 tsp salt
1 tsp red chilli powder
½ tsp turmeric
½ tsp jeera
2 tsp coriander, cracked
2 tsp ginger, chopped
½ cup besan
1 egg
1 tbsp lemon juice

2 tbsp green coriander, chopped
2 tbsp ghee

For the Salsa
1 cup mango, finely chopped
¼ cup onions, finely chopped
1 tbsp green chillies, chopped
1 tbsp green coriander, chopped
3 tbsp lemon juice
Salt to taste
Pepper powder to taste

Apply salt to raw papaya and potato and leave aside for 5 minutes.

Now press them to release water. Put them on a paper towel.

Place them in a large bowl and add all the ingredients except the ghee.

Mix well and shape them into rough, thin patties. Heat a pan and add ghee. When the ghee is hot, cook the patties on both sides evenly.

Serve hot with a mango salsa.

For the salsa, mix all the ingredients and check for seasoning.

Preparation time 20 mins
Cooking time 10 mins

Falafel Serves 2

When I worked in the Gulf I was taken aback by the simple and delicious cuisine it offers. In every nook and corner you can find hot shawarmas, falafels, and fresh bread shops jostling for space. You just can't get bored of these delectable treats. I learnt this chickpea kebab recipe from a local street shop in the Old Kuwait City, which has one of the longest queues I've ever seen.

2 ½ cups **dried chickpeas (safed choley)**
½ cup **onion, chopped**
6 to 7 **garlic cloves**
1 cup **parsley or coriander, chopped**
2 tsp **cumin powder**
2 tsp **coriander powder**
1 tsp **red chili powder**
2 tbsp **refined flour**
Pepper powder to taste
Salt to taste
Oil for frying

Wash and soak the chickpeas overnight. Drain all the excess water the next morning.

Add all the ingredients to the chickpeas and put them in a processor. Churn it into a rough paste. Take care not to make it too smooth.

Remove and mix the paste properly. Wet your hands and make balls of the mixture.

Heat oil in a pan till it is just about hot and deep fry the balls till crisp on the outside.

Remove and serve with tahini sauce*.

For tahini sauce recipe see p 47

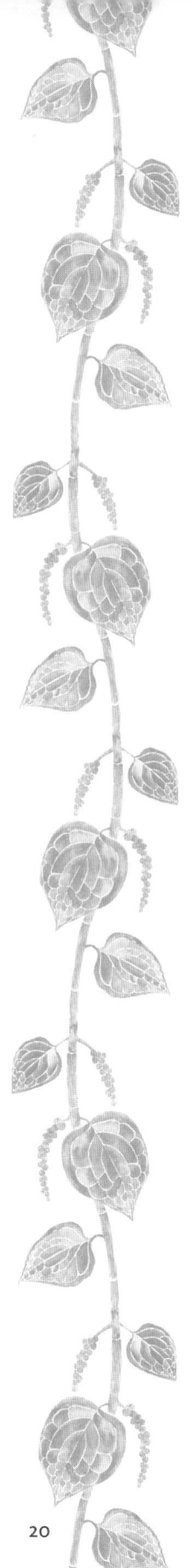

Preparation time **20 mins**
Cooking time **10 mins**

Pea and Potato Croquette Serves 4

This all-time favourite tit-bit is similar to an aloo tikki—the Indian avatar of the French croquette. A croquette has a very smooth silky texture inside and a crisp outer skin, courtesy the breadcrumbs. Made from potatoes, the croquette can adapt to any flavour and filling of your choice. Vegetables, meats, and cheeses easily blend in as a stuffing for the versatile croquette.

2 cups potato, boiled and mashed
1 cup green peas, boiled and mashed
A pinch of nutmeg
2 tbsp milk
20 cheese mozzarella cubes
(1 cm x 1 cm)
½ cup green onions, chopped
1 tbsp refined flour
2 eggs

Oil for frying
Salt to taste
Pepper to taste

For Crumbing
2 eggs
Refined flour for rolling
Dry breadcrumbs for rolling

Place the mashed potato and peas in a bowl, and add salt, pepper, nutmeg, milk, green onions, flour, and 2 eggs. Mix them well and refrigerate for 15 minutes.

Now roll them into equal-sized balls. Stuff each of them with cheese. Shape them into oblong bits.

Place flour, beaten eggs, and breadcrumbs separately in different plates. Cover each potato croquette with flour and dunk them in beaten eggs. After which give them a good roll in the breadcrumbs.

Heat oil to medium hot and deep fry the croquettes till they are crisp golden brown. Remove to a paper towel and serve.

If you do not want to use eggs, you can use an extra 2 tbsp of milk instead in the mixture. And you can avoid eggs in the crumbing process too.

Preparation time 15 mins

Hummus: 3 Ways Serves 2

Hummus is a dip made of chickpea puree. It is extremely versatile and easy to make. Add whatever flavour you want to it as it blends without any fuss. Try herbs, grilled vegetables, or fruits of your choice. It is an ideal base that you can whip up for get togethers with friends and family. Here I give you three different ways to prepare humus.

For Traditional Hummus
2 cups chickpeas, boiled
5 to 6 garlic cloves
½ cup lemon juice
2 tsp cumin powder
Salt to taste
3 tbsp tahini
A pinch of red chilli powder
4 tbsp virgin olive oil

For Hummus Beiruti
¼ cup mint leaves, chopped
¼ cup parsley, chopped
1 green chilli, chopped
1 tbsp onion, chopped (optional)

For Hummus with
Red Peppers and Parsley
1 red capsicum (medium size)
¼ cup parsley, chopped
1 tbsp olive oil
Toasted pine nuts for garnishing (optional)

Method for Traditional Hummus
Place the boiled chickpeas in a blender. Add garlic, lemon juice, cumin powder, 2 tbsp of olive oil, salt, and tahini. Blend till it is creamy and fluffy.

Put the mixture into a bowl. Make a depression using a ladle and pour in the remaining olive oil.

Garnish with a few boiled chickpeas and sprinkle red chilli powder. Serve with hot breads of your choice. Pita* or khaboos is the classic accompaniment.

For Hummus Beiruti follow the above recipe. Mix in chopped parsley, mint, and green chilly.

Method for Hummus with Red Pepper and Parsley
Drizzle a little oil over the red capsicum and roast it over an open flame till the outer skin is charred. Put the capsicum in cold water and remove skin and seeds. Puree this capsicum with traditional hummus and garnish with chopped parsley.

For pita recipe see p 91

Preparation time **20 mins**

Melon n' Cheese Serves 4

Opposites attract. And nothing establishes this fact more than this recipe, which is a perfect balance of two opposites. A classic combination of how the earthy melon complements the rich, deep smokiness of cheese. An easy-peasy recipe that is scrumptious and will leave you wanting more. So much more.

16 **watermelon discs**
4 tbsp **cream cheese**
1 tbsp **mayonnaise**
1 tbsp **virgin olive oil**

Mint leaves for garnishing
A pinch of crushed black pepper
Toasted walnuts for garnishing

Mix the cream cheese and mayonnaise together.

Place the watermelon discs on a platter and add a dollop of cream cheese.

Garnish with mint and toasted walnuts. Drizzle olive oil and sprinkle some pepper.

Raw Papaya Kebabs with Mango Salsa (pg 18)

Hummus: 3 ways (pg 21)

Shish Taouk (pg 23)

Melon n' Cheese (pg 24)

Mini Cheese Calzones (pg 26)

Baked Potato Skins (pg 27)

Preparation time 20 mins
Cooking time 5 mins

Fried Mozzarella Sticks with Tomato Sauce Serves 4

This is a quick tit-bit for cheese lovers. Lightly crumbed cheese sticks is a quick and easy snack on the go, especially for kids.

400 gm **mozzarella cheese**
1 tsp **thyme, dried**
1 tsp **garlic powder (optional)**
¾ cup **refined flour**
¼ cup **cornflour**
2 **eggs**
2 cups **dry breadcrumbs**
Oil for frying
A pinch of salt
A pinch of pepper powder

For the Tomato Sauce
2 tbsp **oil**
2 tbsp **garlic, chopped**
2 tbsp **celery, chopped (optional)**
2 tbsp **onion, chopped**
1 ½ cup **tomatoes, chopped**
½ cup **tomato puree**
1 tsp **red chilli powder**
Salt to taste

Pat dry the cheese using a kitchen towel. Cut the cheese into finger-sized bits. In another bowl, break eggs and mix in 2 tbsp of water and whisk. Mix cornflour and flour in a bowl.

In a separate bowl add breadcrumbs, salt, pepper, garlic powder, and thyme.

Now dunk the cheese in flour and coat evenly. Carefully dunk the cheese in beaten eggs, lift and now dunk in the breadcrumbs. Use clean hands to roll and pat them gently.

Deep fry the cheese sticks in hot oil till they turn golden brown. Strain and place on a kitchen towel.

For the tomato sauce, heat oil and add garlic, celery, and onions together. Sauté till transparent. Now add the chopped tomato, salt, and red chilli powder. Sauté for 3 minutes and add tomato puree. Give it a quick boil for 3 minutes and remove.

Serve hot mozzarella sticks with warm tomato sauce.

Preparation time 45 mins (includes resting time)
Cooking time 15 mins

Mini Cheese Calzones Makes 24 mini calzones

Calzones are very much like an Italian pizza, in fact if you fold a pizza with all its toppings and sauces and bake it, it will be a calzone…well almost. The best part about them is that they're easy to 'carry n eat'. When shaped really small they make an excellent snack. You can fill them with whatever you like. Try various vegetables, meats, cheese, herbs, or eggs.

For the Pizza Dough
500 gm flour
5 gm fresh yeast or 8 gm dry yeast
5 gm sugar
5 gm salt
25 ml olive oil
50 gm sooji
250 ml water
2 eggs

For the Filling
1 cup mozzarella cheese, grated
1 cup Gouda cheese, grated
½ cup onion, diced
½ cup tomatoes, chopped
¼ cup basil, chopped
½ cup green capsicum, chopped
Salt to taste

Place the yeast in a bowl and add ½ cup lukewarm water. Add sugar and 2 tbsp of flour. Mix and leave aside for 15 minutes in a warm place to start the fermentation process.

Once bubbles appear in the mixture, pour in the remaining flour, add salt, olive oil and remaining water and knead into a dough. Now leave this dough covered in a warm place for 20 minutes so that it ferments and doubles in size. Punch the dough back and shape into 24 equal balls. Leave aside for 15 minutes.

For the filling, combine both the cheese and add all vegetables and season with salt.

Now sprinkle some semolina on a flat counter and flatten the individual dough till ½ cm thick. Place the filling in the centre and apply a little water on the edges of the dough. Fold the dough like a half moon and pinch to seal the sides.

Throw in some semolina on a baking tray and place the calzones on them. Whisk eggs and using a brush lightly coat the top of the calzones. Bake in a preheated oven for 12 to 15 minutes at 180°C.
Serve warm with ketchup.

Preparation time 20 mins
Cooking time 60 mins

Baked Potato Skins Serves 4

Baking a raw potato brings out its deep, earthy flavour, which you don't get when you boil it. A bit of magic happens when potato, cheese, and onions combine. Easy to prepare and carry with you, baked potato skins are something that everyone will enjoy, especially the kids. Use vegetables, herbs, or meats or anything else that you may like as the filling.

4 potatoes, medium-sized but long
1 ½ tbsp butter
1 cup Cheddar cheese
½ cup spring onions, chopped

4 tbsp red capsicum, chopped
1 cup sour cream
Salt to taste
Pepper to taste

Clean the potatoes and prick them with a fork. In a preheated oven, bake these potatoes at 200°C till they are cooked all the way through to the centre. It may take about 40 minutes.

Now remove the potatoes and allow them to cool enough to handle them. Cut them in half, length wise. Use a small spoon to scoop out the potato leaving a substantial layer towards the skin.

Now baste the potato both skin side and the inside with butter. Place it back in the oven for 10 minutes at 190°C so that the skin turns crisp.

In the mean time, add grated cheese, spring onion, salt, pepper, and chopped red capsicum to the scooped out potato to make a filling.

Remove the crispy potato skins from the oven and place this filling in the centre. Place the potato skins back in the oven for another 5 to 7 minutes or till the cheese melts.

Remove and serve immediately with sour cream.

Preparation time **20 mins**
Cooking time **10 mins**

Spinach and Cheese Stuffed Mushrooms Serves 4

A few varieties of mushrooms can be very expensive and hard to find in India. This recipe uses the most common variety in India, button mushrooms, and makes an excellent tit-bit for a cocktail party.

20 button mushrooms
¼ cup spinach, blanched and chopped
4 tbsp cream cheese
1 tbsp spring onions, chopped
½ tsp red chilli powder
1 tsp Nigella seeds
1 cup refined flour
2 eggs
2 cups breadcrumbs
Salt to taste

Wash the mushrooms thoroughly in cold water. Snap the stem and chop it finely.

Place the chopped stems in a bowl, along with the spinach, cream cheese, spring onions, Nigella seeds, red chilli powder, and salt.

Using a small spoon, stuff the mushrooms with this mixture. Dunk the mushroom in refined flour, then cover with beaten eggs and roll them in breadcrumbs. Pat gently and fry in hot oil till crisp.

Serve hot.

Preparation time 20 mins
Cooking time 15 mins

Chicken Porcupine Serves 4

This Asian steamed dumpling has raw rice rolled over the chicken mince. Once steamed, the rice puffs and swells resembling a porcupine. It is a delight to look at and equally healthy and delicious to eat.

250 gm **chicken mince**
1 tbsp **garlic, chopped**
3 tbsp **carrots, finely chopped**
3 tbsp **spring onions, finely chopped**
1 tbsp **ginger, finely chopped**
1 tbsp **soya sauce**
1 tbsp **oyster sauce**
1 tsp **sesame oil**
1 tsp **pepper powder**
1 **egg**
½ cup **rice (small, thin grain)**
Oil for greasing
Salt to taste

Wash and soak the rice for 2 hours. Drain the water and keep aside. Place the chicken mince in a bowl. Mix all the ingredients well and divide it into equal-sized balls.

Roll these balls in the soaked raw rice and carefully place these small porcupines on a greased plate. Get the steamer ready and steam these on high heat for 15 minutes.

Remove and serve these cute chicken porcupines with soy sauce on the side.

Preparation time 20 mins
Cooking time 10 mins

Mutton Varuval Serves 4

Varuval means 'fried' in South India. It does not necessarily mean deep fried and can be shallow fried or stir fried as well. This warm and spicy mutton dish is enhanced by the elements of fennel and pepper. A perfect snack for meat lovers.

400 gm mutton cubes
1 cup coconut, grated
6 garlic cloves
½ cup onion, chopped
2 tbsp ginger, chopped
2 tsp cumin
2 tsp fennel
5 peppercorns
2 sprigs of curry leaves

1 tbsp lemon juice
1 tsp turmeric
½ tsp red chilli powder
1 tbsp coriander powder
2 tsp mustard seeds
2 dry red chillies
½ cup coconut oil
2 tbsp fresh coriander
Salt to taste

In a thick-bottomed pan, heat coconut oil and add dry red chillies. Now add mustard seeds and curry leaves. Immediately add the mutton cubes. Sauté on a low heat for 5 minutes and then add turmeric, salt, red chilli powder, and coriander powder.

Add 5 cups of water and cover. Cook till it is three-fourths done.

Separately grind together coconut, cumin, fennel, peppercorn, garlic, onion, and ginger. Once the mutton is three-fourths done, add this paste and cook on a high flame. Stir continuously. Cook till the masala sticks to the mutton.

Check for seasoning and drizzle lemon juice. Garnish with fresh coriander.

Preparation time **10 mins**
Cooking time **10 mins**

Mushroom and Walnuts on Crisp Bread Serves 2

Creamy mushrooms and crunchy walnuts combine to make an excellent starter that will go very well with wines and can also be enjoyed by kids. The flavour of mushrooms is enhanced by the butter, garlic, and thyme.

8 slices **of bread**
1 ½ tbsp **butter**
1 tbsp **garlic, chopped**
1 ½ cup **mushrooms, sliced**
2 tbsp **onions, chopped**
A sprig of thyme
¼ cup **walnuts, toasted**

2 tbsp **parsley, chopped**
½ cup **cherry tomatoes**
½ tbsp **flour**
½ cup **milk**
Salt to taste
Pepper to taste

Apply a little butter on the bread slices and toast them on both sides till crisp. Cut the bread into two bite size pieces.

In a pan, heat butter and sauté the onions and garlic. Add thyme and then the sliced mushrooms. Add salt and pepper and toss the mushrooms till all the moisture evaporates.

Add flour and sauté till blonde, and then pour in the milk. Allow it to thicken.

Now add the walnuts and cherry tomatoes. Toss for a minute and add parsley. Take this off the flame and spoon the mixture onto the crisp bread. Serve immediately.

Preparation time **10 mins**
Cooking time **15 mins**

Quesadilla Serves 4

You cannot get more Mexican than quesadillas—a much-loved dish the world over. Quesadillas are flat breads (flour tortilla generally) that sandwich warm cheese, meat, and vegetables, making a delectable mouthful. It is best served with sour cream and guacamole. A quick and delicious snack for all.

4 **tortilla breads***
2 tbsp **oil**
1 cup **mozzarella cheese**, grated
1 cup **Cheddar cheese**, grated
1 cup **onions**, diced
1 cup **tomatoes**, diced
2 cups **chicken**, boiled and diced

½ cup **olives**, sliced
½ cup **jalapenos**, sliced
1 cup **capsicum**, diced
2 tbsp **coriander**, chopped
Salt to taste
Pepper powder to taste

Heat a thick-bottomed pan on medium heat and pour in some oil. Place a flour tortilla in the pan and spread the mozzarella and Cheddar cheese on top of it.

Sprinkle the rest of the vegetables in and flatten them gently, spreading them around the tortilla at the same time. Sprinkle salt, pepper, and chopped coriander.

Now carefully fold the tortilla in a half moon shape. Cook on both sides till crisp.

Remove and cut in equal triangles. Serve while it is still hot with guacamole and sour cream.

*Note: For tortilla recipe see p 86

Preparation time 10 mins
Cooking time 15 mins

Flat Bread with Pesto and Cottage Cheese (Paneer) Serves 4

The best flavours are often simple. The magic of fresh basil and olive oil is eternal and can be relished with freshly baked, lightly salted bread. An all-time simple snack, which can also make an appearance at a cocktail party.

350 gm **fermented dough***
5 tbsp **pesto (see pg 52)**
1 cup **paneer, crumbled**

Salt to taste
Pepper to taste

Divide the dough into equal portions and roll it out into an oval shape about ½ cm thick. Bake in a hot oven at 180°C for 5 minutes.

When it is done, remove and smear pesto over it. Add the crumbled paneer and sprinkle salt and pepper.

Bake it again for 5 minutes at the same temperature or till the bread is fully baked.

Remove and cut into smaller pieces and serve.

*For fermented dough use the calzone recipe.

Preparation time **15 mins**
Cooking time **10 mins**

Lotus Stem Crisps (Kurkuri Kamal Kakdi) Serves 2

Lotus stem can be used in many ways. In India, it is used to make kebabs and also used in curries. Often, it is added to meat dishes as it absorbs its flavour well and gives a great crunch to the dish. When thinly sliced and fried, lotus stem can make an excellent snack. It can be preserved in an air-tight container for a few days.

10 **lotus stems**
½ cup **cornstarch**
2 tsp **chaat masala**
½ tsp **red chilli powder**
Oil for frying
Salt to taste

Peel the lotus stems and slice them into thin wafers (use a slicer for maximum effect). Immerse them in water to remove impurities. Strain and pat dry properly and then coat them in cornstarch thoroughly.

Heat oil and deep fry the lotus stems till they are crisp. Remove and immediately sprinkle with chaat masala and red chilli powder.

Preparation time 20 mins
Cooking time 20 mins

Crispy Shredded Lamb (Gosht ki Sev) Serves 2

Hyderabad has added great richness and flavour to India's culinary history. This is a time consuming recipe and requires some patience, but the reward is more than satisfying. Thin shreds of deep fried mutton eaten as a snack was a nawabi favourite of the bygone era. This dish makes for a perfect snack for parties and cocktails.

250 gm **mutton chunks (2"thick)**
½ tsp **turmeric**
1 tbsp **ginger paste**
1 ½ **garlic paste**
¾ tsp **red chilli powder**
2 tsp **dry mango powder**
½ cup **cornstarch**
Oil to fry
Salt to taste

In a pressure cooker, combine mutton, salt, turmeric, ginger and garlic paste. Add sufficient water. Pressure-cook the mutton till it is very soft. Remove mutton pieces and place them on the kitchen counter.

Place a cloth on the hot mutton chunks (be careful to protect your hand) and apply pressure from the top. Now carefully pull out the fibers of the meat like shreds.

Mix the shreds with cornflour and fry it in medium hot oil till they are crisp. Remove them to a kitchen paper and allow them to rest.

Sprinkle red chilli powder, dry mango powder, and little salt. Toss gently and serve.

Preparation time **10 mins**
Cooking time **15 mins**

Golden Fried Prawns Serves 4

During my training period in the Chinese kitchen at the Taj, I came across this unique dish that used soda water for the batter. As a trainee, the process of making the batter with soda water intrigued me. The resulting batter is light and crisp when fried and can also be used to fry vegetables like babycorn.

20 **prawns (medium size)**
Oil for frying
Refined flour for dusting

For the Marinade
1 tbsp **soya sauce**
1 **green chilli**, chopped
1 tbsp **oyster sauce**

1 tbsp **garlic**, chopped
1 tsp **sesame oil**

For the Batter
1 cup **refined flour**
1 cup **cornflour**
¾ cup **soda water**

For the batter, mix together cornflour and refined flour and pour in the soda water to make a thick batter. Mix and keep aside.

Clean the prawns and keep the tail on. Run a knife slightly on the back of the prawn to straighten it out. Pat dry and keep aside.

In a bowl, mix together soya sauce, oyster sauce, green chilli, garlic, and sesame oil. Marinate the prawns in this mixture for 10 minutes.

Now dunk the prawns in the flour and hold them by their tail and dip them in the batter.

Deep fry the prawns in hot oil till they are golden brown. Serve hot with remaining marinade.

Preparation time 10 mins
Cooking time 20 mins

Shammi Kebabs Serves 4

Shammi kebabs are a household name in India. It is essentially a minced mutton/lamb kebab that is twice cooked. The lentil blends with the mutton to give it an inimitable taste. Savour this meaty kebab with a roomali roti.

250 gm **mutton/lamb mince**
¼ cup **lentil channa dal**
½ cup **onion, diced**
2 tbsp **ginger, chopped**
1 ½ tbsp **garlic, chopped**
1 **dry red chilli**
1 **green chilli, slit**

2 tsp **black cumin (shahi jeera)**
1 **cinnamon (½" long)**
1 **black cardamom**
1 tsp **salt**
1 tsp **turmeric**
500 ml **water**
2 tbsp **oil**

Wash and soak the channa dal for 10 minutes. Now mix all the ingredients except oil and put it on medium heat. Remove scum as and when it surfaces.

Boil till the dal and mutton are cooked and the water has almost evaporated. Remove and allow it to cool.

In a mixer/mincer, mince this meat thoroughly into a paste. Remove and allow it to cool; check for seasoning.

Make round patties and shallow fry in hot oil till both sides are crisp and brown. Serve hot.

Preparation time **15 mins**
Cooking time **45 mins**

Asparagus and Cherry Tomato Cheese Tarts Serves 6

Tarts are very close to my heart. The design and shape of a tart is so pretty to look at that it automatically invites you to pick it up and eat it. Tarts can be sweet or savoury. Asparagus and cheery tomatoes are a harmonious balance of colour and taste. Bake these tiny tarts for a cocktail party and large ones to share with family and friends.

For the Tart
220 gm **refined flour**
100 gm **butter (salted)**
80 ml (approx) **chilled water**

For the Filling
10 **asparagus**
10 **cherry tomatoes**

300 ml **cream**
2 **eggs**
A sprig of **rosemary**
A pinch of **nutmeg**
1 ½ cup **Cheddar or Gouda cheese,** grated
Pepper powder to taste
Salt to taste

Rub the flour and butter together till you get a nice crumbly texture. Now add chilled water to make the dough. Knead it well, cover and place in the fridge for 15 minutes.

Peel the asparagus and blanch it in boiling water. Immediately plunge it into cold water. Mix eggs, cream, grated cheese, pepper powder, nutmeg, rosemary, and a little salt.

Remove the dough from the fridge and roll it out flat about ½ cm thick. Using a rolling pin, lift the dough and place over the tart mould. Gently cover the mould and push the dough towards all edges of the mould so that it blankets it well. Press gently on the top to cut off excess dough. Prick with a fork and bake in a hot oven at 200°C for 5 to 7 minutes. Remove and place the asparagus and cherry tomatoes inside the tart.

Now gently pour the egg and cream mixture into the tart. Carefully lift and bake in the oven at 180°C for 30 minutes. If the tart mould is small then it might bake quicker. Insert a knife in between, if it is clean then it is cooked.

Remove from oven and allow it to rest for 5 minutes. Carefully remove and cut into slices to serve.

Chicken Porcupine (pg 29)

Queso Fundido (pg 32)

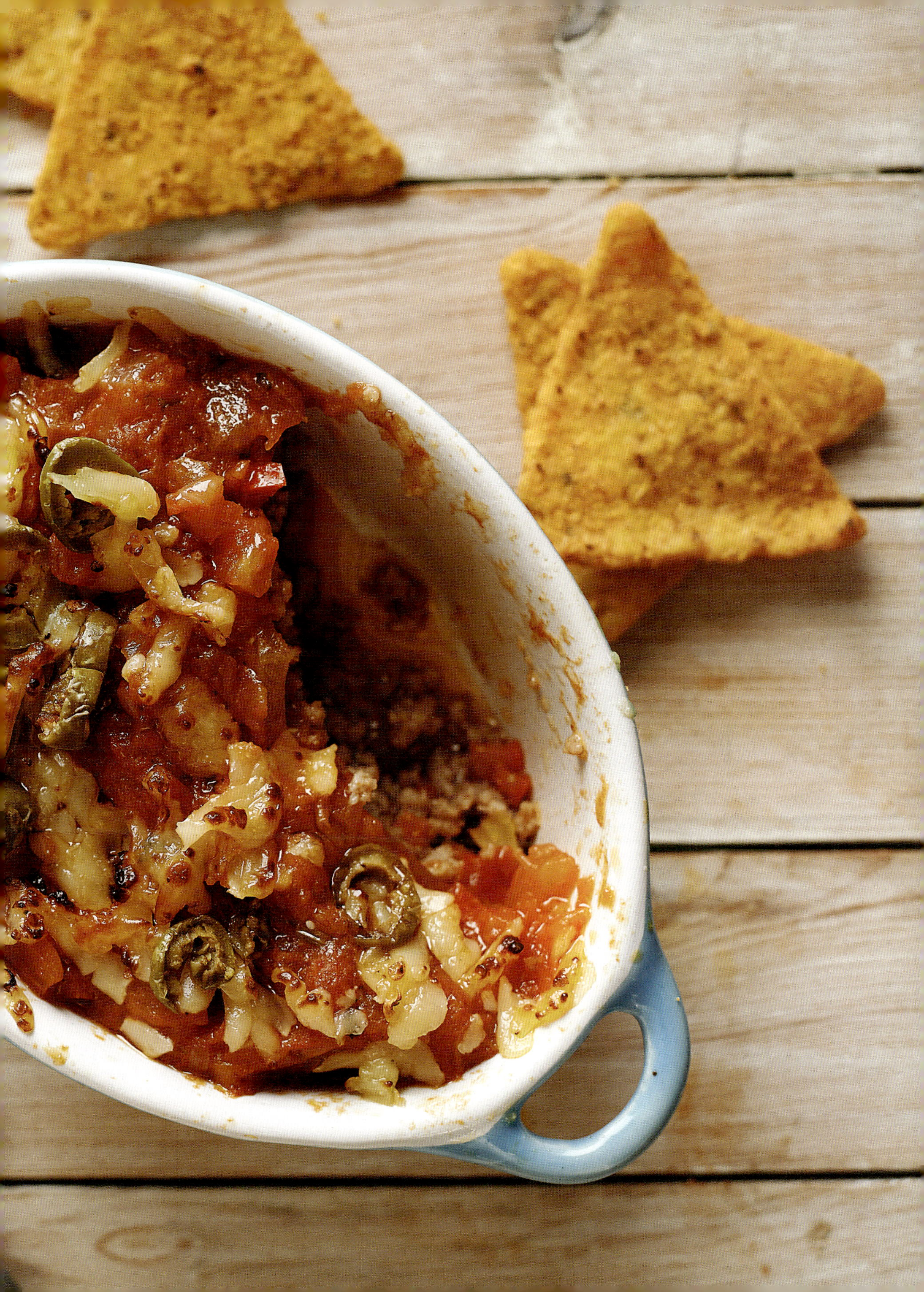

Harissa Marinated Grilled Prawns (pg 33)

Quesadilla (pg 34)

Asparagus and Cherry Tomato Cheese Tarts (pg 40)

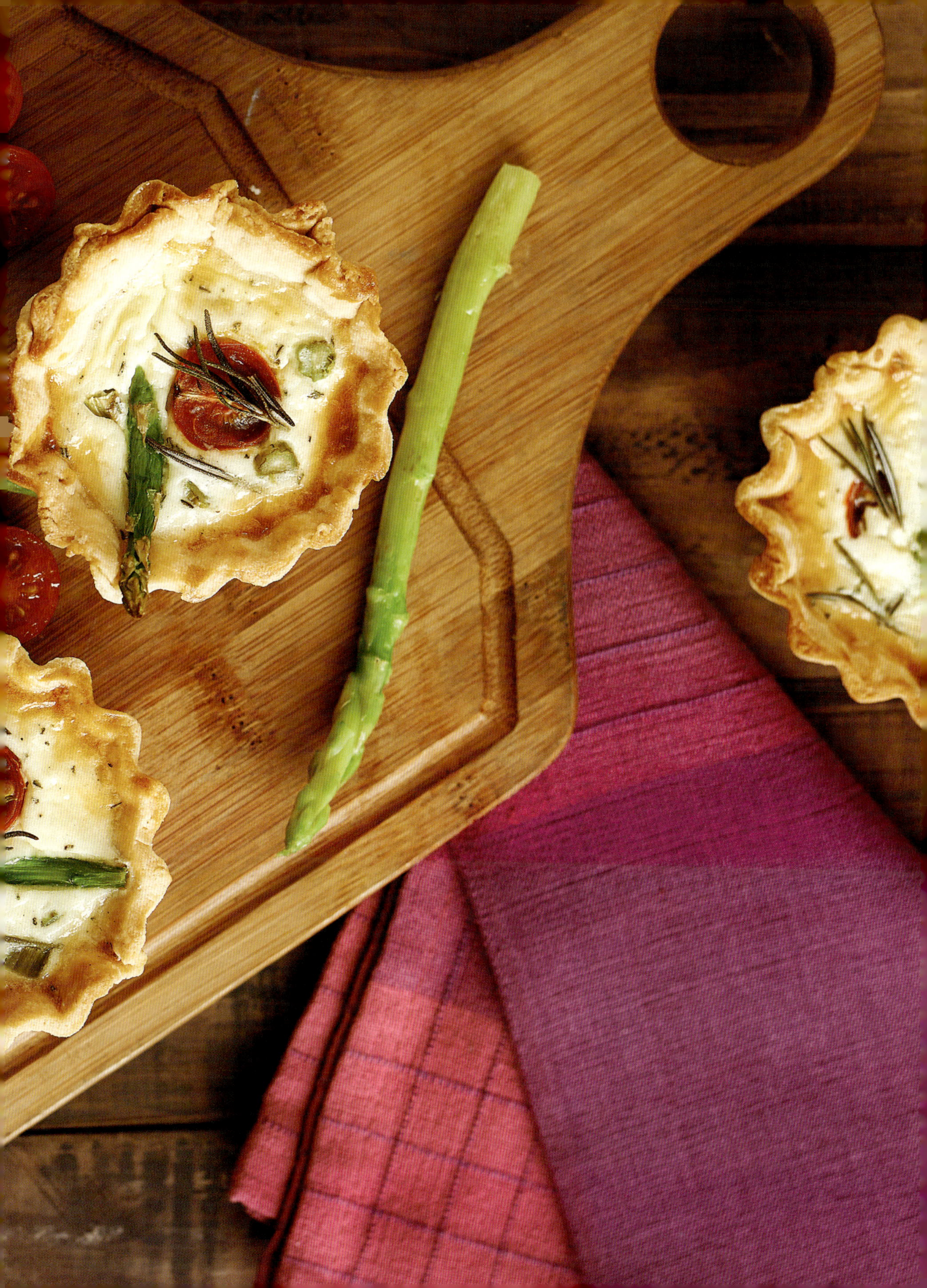

Fried Fish Amritsari (pg 42)

Preparation time 15 mins
Cooking time 15 mins

Keerai Vadai Serves 6

'Keerai' is a local leafy spinach and 'vadai' is the patty. I learnt this dish at Southern Spice—the award winning restaurant at Taj Coromandel, Chennai, during my days of training in the southern kitchens.

2 cups **channa dal (soaked)**
1 tbsp **fennel seeds**
12 **peppercorns**
1 tbsp **cumin**
½ tsp **asafoetida (heeng)**
1 **green chilli, chopped**

2 cups **spinach leaves, chopped**
1 cup **onions, chopped**
12 **curry leaves**
Oil for frying
Salt to taste

Drain the water completely out of the soaked dal and put it in the grinder.

Add cumin, peppercorns, fennel seeds, curry leaves, and green chilly. Grind to a coarse paste. Use very little water if at all required.

Remove the paste in a bowl and add heeng, salt, and chopped spinach.

Wet your hands using water and make small discs of the mixture.

Deep fry them in medium hot oil till golden brown. Serve with coconut chutney.

Preparation time 15 mins
Cooking time 15 mins

Fried Fish Amritsari Serves 2

A lot has been written about this style of fried fish which comes from Amritsar, Punjab. For the longest time in my career, I was serving this fish all wrong. For some strange reason this fish ends up on tables in a deep red colour, but a true Amritsari style fish does not use Kashmiri red chillies or red colour. It is a simple dish, one that doesn't use any batter. The fish used is almost always Singhara/Catfish or Surmai/King Fish.

250 gm fish fillet
Salt to taste
A pinch of asafoetida
1 tsp red chilli powder
1 ½ tbsp lemon juice
1 tbsp ginger paste
1 tbsp garlic paste

2 tbsp flour
2 tbsp besan
2 tsp ajwain
2 tsp chaat masala*
Oil for frying
A few lemon wedges

Pat dry the fish and cut into smaller pieces. Apply salt, red chilli powder, lemon juice, ajwain, heeng, ginger paste, and garlic paste. Let it rest for 15 minutes.

Now apply flour and besan. Rub it properly on the fish. Heat oil and deep fry the fish in medium hot oil till it is crisp. Serve with lemon wedges, sliced onions, and mint chutney.

*Chaat masala is a sour and spicy mixture of masalas that you can easily buy at any Indian store.

The Essentials: Condiments, Dips, Relishes, Chutneys

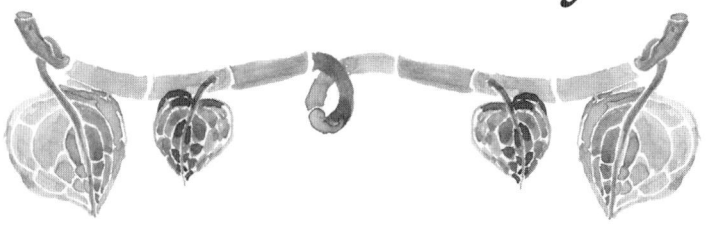

Preparation time 15 mins
Cooking time 10 mins

Red Chilli Paste Makes 1 cup

This tasty and versatile paste is made with chillies and seasoning. It can be used as a marinade, dip, or as a flavouring agent. Remember to use gloves or wash your hands after handling so much chilli.

250 gm **dry red chillies**
200 gm **tomato ketchup**
200 ml **white vinegar**
15 gm **sugar**

300 ml **oil**
30 gm **ginger,** chopped
30 gm **garlic,** chopped
Salt to taste

Boil the chillies in sufficient water. Drain the water and make a thick paste out of it. Heat oil in a pan, sauté garlic and ginger till golden brown.

Add chilli paste and cook it on slow flame until all the moisture evaporates. Now add tomato ketchup, white vinegar, sugar, and salt. Cook till the oil separates and appears on the top. Cool and use as required.

Preparation time 10 mins
Cooking time 5 mins

Pineapple Chutney Serves 2

This sweet and sour chutney is a refreshing accompaniment on a hot summer afternoon. Remember, a good chutney never hides the true flavour of its main ingredient.

1 ½ cup **pineapple,** diced
¾ cup **sugar**
1 tsp **red chilli powder**

½ tsp **salt**
½ tsp **black salt**
½ cup **vinegar**

Mix all the ingredients and cook for 12 minutes on low heat. Once it thickens remove and allow it to cool.

Preparation time **10 mins**

Tahini Makes 1 cup

This simple paste of sesame seeds with olive oil is used in various Arabic preparations. It is easily available in stores and even easier to prepare and store. You can refrigerate it for a long time. Tahini is used to make tahini sauce, which is a thinner and used as an accompaniment.

2 cups **sesame seeds**
¾ cup **olive oil**

Mix the sesame seeds and olive oil and blend into a fine smooth paste.

Preparation time **10 mins**

Tahini Sauce Makes 1 cup

Tahini sauce has a pungent flavour of sesame and should be sparingly used. It can be used as a dipping sauce with starters from Middle Eastern cuisine. Simple to make and lovely to taste!

1 cup **tahini**
Salt to taste
½ cup **lemon juice**

2 tsp **garlic paste**
2 tbsp **olive oil**

Mix all the ingredients together and refrigerate before using. Your tahini sauce is ready!

Preparation time 15 mins
Cooking time 15 mins

Aubergine and Peanut Chutney *Makes 1 small jar*

This unique recipe is somewhat similar to the Hyderabadi dish of sweet and sour eggplants. Together the sourness of the tamarind and the sweetness of jaggery combine to make a great flavour.

6 cups aubergine, diced
½ cup olive oil
2 tsp kalonji
1 tbsp jeera
¼ cup curry leaves
2 cups tomatoes, chopped

2 tsp red chilli powder
1 tsp turmeric
2 cups jiggery, grated
1 cup tamarind pulp
½ cup peanuts, roasted
Salt to taste

Heat olive oil and add kalonji and jeera. When it crackles, add curry leaves and immediately add the tomatoes. Sauté for a minute. Add red chilli powder, turmeric, and salt. Stir for a minute.

Now add the aubergines and cook for 3 to 4 minutes. Add tamarind, cover and let it simmer on low heat for 2 to 3 minutes. Add the grated jaggery and roasted peanuts. Check for seasoning.

Remove and allow it to cool. Store in a tight fitting jar.

From top: Sour Cream (pg 46), Guacamole (pg 53)

From top: Tahini Sauce (pg 45), Toum (pg 50), Tzatziki (pg 46)

From top: Pesto (pg 54), Charmoula Sauce (pg 47), Olive Tapenad (pg 49)

Lemon Water Pickle (pg 52)

Pineapple Chutney (pg 44)

Coconut Chutney (pg 47)

Tahini (pg 45)

Aubergine and Peanut Chutney (pg 48)

Preparation time **20 mins**

Olive Tapenade Makes 1 ½ cup

The French make a very fine chopped mash of olives, capers, anchovies, and olive oil and use this over toasted breads as marinades or as a rub. A delicious way to enjoy bread.

2 cups **green olives, seedless**
1 cup **black olives, seedless**
5 **anchovies, canned**
½ cup **capers**

4 **garlic cloves**
2 tbsp **lemon juice**
3 tbsp **virgin olive oil**
Pepper powder to taste

Place all the ingredients in a blender and make it into a coarse paste. Alternatively chop up everything very fine and mix in olive oil. Refrigerate immediately. Use as a dip, spread, or a filling, and you can also serve it on crisp toast.

If you wish to make a vegetarian tapenade, then omit the anchovies.

Preparation time 10 mins

Toum
(Lebanese Garlic Sauce) Makes 2 cups

Toum is a sauce prepared in the Levante cuisine and makes for a great tasting accompaniment for grilled meats.

1 ½ cup **big garlic cloves, peeled***
½ cup **lemon juice**

4 cups **olive oil (or any neutral cooking oil)**
1 tsp **salt**

In a dry and clean food processor, place the garlic cloves and salt. Churn the garlic and keep scrapping the sides. Keep the food processor running and add oil in a thin stream, little by little.

Once half the oil is used, add half of the lemon juice, little by little. Turn off the processor, scrape the sides and put it on again.

Repeat the process of pouring oil and then lemon juice till the sauce is white and fluffy. If you do it too quickly or pour in more oil, the sauce will curdle/split. In this case, don't throw the curdled sauce. Clean the food processor and add some more garlic and salt, then slowly add the curdled sauce little by little till it all comes together.

Refrigerate and serve with kebabs.

*This recipe works best with big garlic cloves which are easier to peel and less pungent that the small ones. If you're using the smaller variety, then about a cup of it will do.

Preparation time **10 mins**

Mint and Spring Onion Chutney Makes 1 cup

A lovely fresh chutney that gives a zing to every bite. Serve it with kebabs and watch the magic happen. The flavour of mint is especially well released if prepared in a mortar pestle.

4 cups **mint leaves**
1 cup **spring onions, chopped**
4 **garlic cloves, crushed**
1 **green chilli**

4 tbsp **tamarind pulp**
Water as required
Salt to taste

Mix boiled and cooled water in tamarind pulp to make it runny and thin.

In a mortar, add the mint leaves, spring onions, chilli, and garlic. Crush them roughly with a pestle. Remove to a bowl and add the tamarind pulp. Season with salt and serve.

If you are using a blender, add a few ice cubes to keep the temperature of the chutney cold.

Preparation time **10 mins**

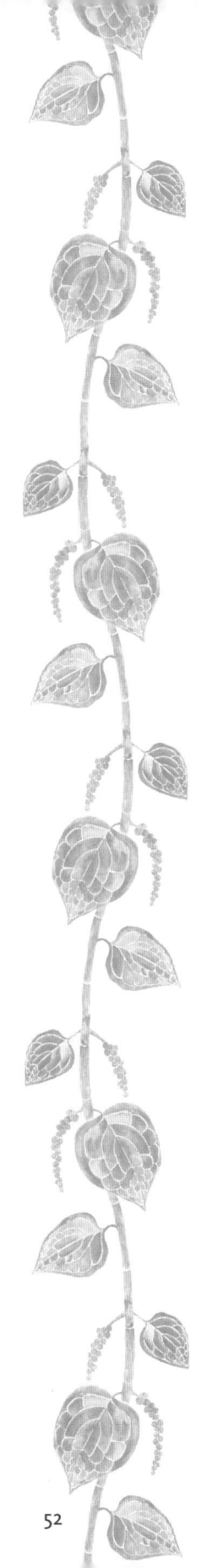

Churan Chutney Makes 1 ½ cup

Traditionally, churan is considered to be a good digestive and consumed just as it is or with vegetables like bitter gourd and okra. The main ingredients of this spice are dried mango powder, salt, and roasted cumin. You can find churan in most Indian stores.

1 ½ cup **churan**	½ cup **dried mango powder**
1 cup **water**	Black **salt** to taste
½ cup **sugar**	1 tbsp **roasted cumin powder**
1 tsp **red chilli powder**	

Combine all the ingredients and give it a boil. Remove, let it cool, and serve with any starter of your choice.

Preparation time **10 mins**

Lemon Water Pickle Makes 1 large jar

This style of pickling lemons in water is prevalent in Middle Eastern cuisine. This pickle is oil-free and that makes it light and fresh.

10 **lemons** (large ones for pickling)	2 **bay leaves**
1 litre **vinegar**	½ cup **salt**
500 ml **water**	1 ½ cup **sugar**
10 **peppercorns**	

Slit the large lemons criss-cross from the top. In a pan, mix vinegar, water, peppercorns, salt, sugar, and bay leaves. Give it a boil and allow it to cool completely.

Place the lemons in a clean and dry glass jar. Pour the pickling solution on top and cover. You can use it after 20 days.

Preparation time **10 mins**

Mayonnaise Makes 2 cups

Mayonnaise needs no introduction, but when freshly prepared it imparts a taste that is unmatched.

2 **egg yolks**
½ tsp **salt**
2 tsp **mustard paste**
1 tbsp **lemon juice**
250 ml **oil**

In a clean, dry bowl place the egg yolks. Add mustard paste, salt, and lemon juice and start whisking it.

Now, very slowly pour the oil in a thin stream into the mixture. Keep whisking it continuously. You might want an extra hand to help you pour the oil while you keep whisking.

Emulsify the entire oil by gently whisking it. Once done, transfer the mayonnaise in a clean bowl and refrigerate.

Preparation time **10 mins**

Guacamole Makes 1 cup

Guacamole is a sauce/dip made from fresh avocadoes. Avocadoes are a super food that has great health benefits and the beauty of this fruit is that it really does not have a taste of its own. It blends into whatever you add them to it.

4 **avocadoes**
4 tbsp **lemon juice**
¼ cup **onions**, chopped
¼ cup **tomatoes**, chopped
¼ cup **coriander**, chopped
2 **garlic cloves**, chopped
Salt to taste

Peel the avocadoes and mash them. Add the rest of the ingredients and mix together. Serve chilled.

Preparation time 10 mins

Pesto Makes 3 cups

Pesto comes from Italy and is probably the best way to use basil. Basil has a delicate flavour and gets accentuated when crushed and mixed with good quality olive oil. Pesto can be served as an accompaniment or used as a marinade or can be added to enhance the flavour of a dish.

3 cups **basil leaves**
¼ cup **pinenuts or walnuts,** lightly toasted
2 **garlic cloves**
Salt to taste
½ cup **olive oil**
½ cup **Parmesan cheese, grated***

In a blender, add basil, garlic, salt, olive oil, and pinenuts. Blend into a coarse paste. Remove and add grated cheese.

*You can use any hard cheese if you cannot get parmesan.

Healthy and Fun Menus for Kids

Preparation time **15 mins**

ABC Smoothie Serves 2

A smoothie, simply put, is blended yoghurt. The Indian equivalent is lassi—a refreshing beverage that has been around ages. ABC or Apple Banana Carrot Smoothie has all the goodness of fruits and vegetables and is a refreshing breakfast drink. Use fruits that you like and blend with yoghurt along with sugar or honey.

3 cups **yoghurt**
1 cup **milk**
2 tbsp **sugar**

1 **apple**, diced
2 cups **bananas**, diced
1 **carrot**, diced

Mix all the ingredients in a blender and churn them into a smoothie. Pour in glasses and serve cold.

Preparation time **15 mins**
Cooking time **5 mins**

French Toast Serves 2

One of the most indulgent breakfast dishes is the French toast. As a kid born and raised in Delhi, I always enjoyed French toast in its simplest avatar—dipped in savory beaten eggs and cooked. At culinary school, I was surprised that there was a sweet version to this—the original way. And once I tasted this magical dish I instantly fell in love with it. I enjoy it especially with chocolate sauce and my choice of seasonal fruits. I use thick bread from a loaf rather than pre-sliced bread.

- 1 tbsp **butter**
- 4 **slices of bread (preferably thick and old)**
- 4 **eggs**
- 1/3 cup **milk**
- ½ tsp **cinnamon powder**
- 1 ½ tbsp **honey**
- 1 cup **banana, sliced**
- 1 cup **berries**
- ½ cup **whipped sweetened cream** (optional)

Break the eggs in a clean bowl. Add milk and cinnamon powder. Whisk it till it is very frothy. Now dip and soak the bread in the eggs for a few seconds*.

Melt butter in a non-stick pan and place the bread and cook on both sides on medium heat. Allow the egg mixture to cook completely and the outside to brown.

Remove to a serving plate and sprinkle sliced bananas and berries. Drizzle honey or whipped cream, over it and serve.

*Remember the thickness and freshness of the bread will decide how long you need to soak it. The thicker and older the bread the more soaking time it will require.

Preparation time 15 mins

Granola Parfait: Two Ways Serves 2

Granola is a breakfast cereal consisting of rolled oats, fruits, and nuts. It may or may not be sweetened. For this recipe you can use mixed breakfast cereals of your choice with nuts.

2 ½ cups **granola**	1 tbsp **honey**
1 cup **yoghurt (thick)**	½ cup **fruits, chopped**
½ tsp **vanilla extract**	3 tbsp **almonds, chopped**
2 tbsp **jam (any)**	2 tbsp **pumpkin seeds**

Whisk the yoghurt with the vanilla extract. In another bowl, whisk the jam.

In 2 separate glasses, add a thin layer of granola. Now add 2 big scoops of yoghurt to both the glasses. In one glass, add a thin layer of jam, then add some chopped almonds. Add some more yogurt and garnish with some almonds.

In the other glass, add chopped fruits and then a thin layer of honey and pumpkin seeds. Add some yoghurt and garnish with pumpkin seeds. Serve immediately.

Use seasonal fruits of your choice. If berries are in season then you are in luck as they add that magic tang to this simple and healthy recipe.

Preparation time 10 mins

Creamy Avocado and Cucumber Soup Serves 4

This cold soup is both refreshing and easy and uses no gas or ovens. Perfect after a hectic day at school or after a big game.

8 ripe avocadoes
1 cucumber
1 garlic clove
2 tbsp lemon juice
2 tsp Madras curry powder

¼ cup mint leaves
6 ice cubes
½ cup cream
Salt to taste
½ tsp black pepper, crushed

In a food processor, purée the avocadoes, cucumber, garlic, lemon, Madras curry powder, mint leaves and a few ice cubes.

Pour out in a bowl and add cream, salt, and pepper. Serve chilled.

Preparation time **10 mins**
Cooking time **12 mins**

Tomatoes and Pickled Beet Salad Serves 2

If you dislike tomatoes and beetroot, I guarantee you will start liking them after you taste this. The colours are vibrant and the pickling makes the beets very interesting.

10 **slices of red tomatoes**
10 **slices of green tomatoes**
10 **cherry tomatoes, halved**
10 **slices of beetroot**
2 **sprigs of basil**
2 **garlic cloves, crushed**

4 **tbsp olive oil**
Salt to taste
Pepper powder to taste
2 **cups vinegar**
1 ½ **cup sugar**

In a pot, add vinegar, ½ cup water, and sugar. Allow it to boil and then add the beets. Cook till beets are tender but still have a bite. Remove from heat and allow them to cool in the same liquid.

Crush basil leaves and add crushed and chopped garlic to it. Then add salt and pepper and whisk in olive oil.

Arrange the tomato and beetroot slices on a tray and sprinkle the dressing on top. Serve immediately.

Preparation time **15 mins**
Cooking time **30 mins**

Baked Mac n' Cheese Serves 2

The tastiest pasta in the world is also the easiest to make. Mac n' Cheese makes the perfect lunchbox dish for your child.

1 cup **macaroni**
3 tbsp **butter**
2 tbsp **flour**
1 cup **milk**
1 **bay leaf**
2 tbsp **onions, chopped**

1 **egg**
Salt to taste
1 cup **Cheddar cheese, grated**
¼ cup **breadcrumbs**
2 tbsp **parsley, chopped**

Boil 6 cups of water and add ½ tsp of salt. Add macaroni and boil till al dente. Strain and keep aside.

In a separate pan, melt 2 tbsp of butter and add bay leaf and onions. Sauté on low heat for 30 seconds and add flour and sauté on low heat for a minute.

Carefully pour the milk and keep whisking to avoid lumps. Cook till milk starts to thicken enough to coat the back of the spoon.

Remove from heat and add grated cheese, macaroni, a pinch of salt, and egg. Mix it well and pour in a baking dish. Mix 1 tbsp of butter with the breadcrumbs and spread it on top of the dish.

In a preheated oven, bake the dish at 180°C for 20 minutes. Remove from oven and sprinkle parsley. Serve hot.

Preparation time **20 mins**

Chocolate Mousse with Citrus Rind Serves 5

Chocolate is my favourite and I love it in almost any form. The citrus adds an interesting touch to this recipe and makes the velvety mousse irresistible.

250 gm **dark chocolate**
25 gm **sugar**
100 ml **milk**

200 gm **whipped cream**
2 tbsp **lemon/orange/sweet lime rind**

Whip chilled cream using a whisk till it is stiff.

Boil milk and sugar, and add chopped chocolate and mix till all lumps are removed. Remove from heat and allow it to cool.

Gently mix (lift and fold) the chocolate in the whipped cream with the rind. Scoop into glasses. Refrigerate for an hour and serve cold.

Preparation time **10 mins**
Cooking time **15 mins**

Cream of Broccoli Soup Serves 4

Creamy broccoli with thyme and molten cheese will fill up that hungry tummy. Make sure you don't overcook the broccoli—what's green should remain green.

4 tbsp **butter**
5 **peppercorns**
1 **bay leaf**
½ cup **onions, chopped**
2 tbsp **garlic, chopped**
A **sprig of thyme**

3 cups **broccoli, chopped**
2 tbsp **flour**
500 ml **milk**
1 cup **Cheddar cheese, grated**
Salt to taste

Heat butter and add peppercorns and bay leaf. Now add onions and garlic and sauté for 3 minutes. Add thyme and broccoli. Sauté for 2 minutes and then add flour. Cook on low heat till the flour turns blonde in colour.

Now add milk and bring it to a boil. Allow it to thicken. Remove from fire, strain, and purée the contents. Put back the purée and add enough water to get it back to a coating consistency and bring it to a quick boil.

Season the soup with grated cheese, and remove immediately. Serve hot.

Preparation time **10 mins**
Cooking time **40 mins**

Baked Chicken and Tomato with Potato Mash Serves 4

Baking has never been so much fun. Remember all those chicken recipes that looked so good in pictures but seemed difficult to make? Well you can now become a real chef and bake chicken with ease.

4 pieces **chicken**
½ tsp **salt**
A pinch of **pepper powder**
2 tsp **thyme**, chopped
1 tbsp **garlic**, chopped
Flour for dusting
4 tbsp **olive oil**
25 **cherry tomatoes**
12 **olives** (whole and pitted)

For the Potato Mash
4 large **potatoes**
2 tbsp **butter**
Salt to taste
Pepper to taste
1/3 cup **milk**

Marinate the chicken with salt, pepper, garlic, thyme, and 2 tbsp olive oil. In the same marinade, add the cherry tomatoes and olives. Allow it to rest for 15 minutes.

Now remove the chicken pieces and dunk them in the flour to coat thinly.

Heat a pan and add the remaining olive oil. Place the chicken in the pan and cook to brown the chicken from the outside and from all sides.

In a baking tray, add the marinated tomatoes and olives, place the chicken and the juices from the pan. Cover and cook in a preheated oven for 30 minutes. Remove and serve hot with tomatoes and olives.

For the mash, peel and cut the potatoes into four. Boil the potatoes with some salt.

Once boiled, immediately strain them. Let it rest in the strainer for a minute, then immediately transfer to a deep pan.

Using a potato masher, mash up the potatoes while they are still hot.

Now add butter and milk to the potato and place it in a pan. Put the pan on medium heat. Season with salt and pepper. Toss till the mash comes together. Serve it with baked chicken.

Preparation time **10 mins**
Cooking time **20 mins**

Baked Yoghurt Serves 2

Baking just got even simpler. This confluence of yoghurt with vanilla and lemon is irresistible. This is a delicious and healthy dessert. Combine it with fresh fruits and fruit sauces for more fun.

125 gm **yoghurt**
125 gm **cream**
100 gm **condensed milk**

1 tsp **vanilla extract**
1 tbsp **lemon rind**
Fresh fruits/fruit sauce (optional)

Whisk together yoghurt, cream, condensed milk, vanilla extract, and lemon rind. Mix them nicely and then pour in individual oven-proof cups.

Place them in a deep roasting tray. Pour water up till half the height of the cups. Bake in a preheated oven at 160°C for 20 to 25 minutes or till it is firm to touch.

Bring to room temperature and then chill them in the refrigerator. You may top it up with fresh fruits or any fruit sauce of your choice.

Preparation time 10 mins
Cooking time 5 mins

Tomato Bruschetta Serves 4

A classic Italian dish that is both simple to make and yum to eat. The taste of fresh tomato and basil is nothing short of divine. This is a quick recipe that you can whip up when your children are celebrating with their friends or for picnics.

8 tomatoes
2 garlic cloves
2 tsp balsamic vinegar*
2 tbsp basil leaves, chopped

2 tbsp virgin olive oil
Salt to taste
Pepper powder to taste
12 French bread slices**

Make two small incisions on the tomatoes and put them in boiling water for 10 seconds. Remove and immediately put them in chilled water. This helps in removing the skin of the tomatoes without cooking them. Now remove the skin, quarter the tomatoes, and remove the seeds.

Chop the tomatoes finely and place them in a bowl. Smash garlic and finely chop it. Add salt, pepper, balsamic vinegar, garlic, chopped basil leaves, and 1 tbsp olive oil to the tomatoes.

Heat a pan on medium heat and place the sliced bread. Apply olive oil and toast it till crisp. Remove and spoon the mixture on top.

*You can substitute balsamic vinegar with lemon juice and French bread with thick sandwich bread.

Preparation time 15 mins
Cooking time 5 mins

Finger Sandwiches: Two Ways Serves 2

What I love about sandwiches is that they can pack almost anything you like. So here are two basic recipes; feel free to innovate and add whatever you like in your sandwiches.

For Grilled Cheese and Onion Sandwich
2 slices of large bread
1 tbsp butter
2 slices onion, sliced horizontally
A pinch of oregano
2 cheese slices

For Pulled Chicken Sandwich
2 slices of large bread
1 cup chicken (boiled and shredded)
1 tbsp mayonnaise
A pinch of salt
A pinch of pepper
1 tsp mustard paste
1 tbsp parsley, chopped
1 tbsp grated cheese
1 tbsp butter

For the grilled cheese sandwich, apply butter on both sides of the bread. On one slice, place the cheese slice, onions, and sprinkle oregano. Place the other slice of bread on top and press.

Place the sandwich in a preheated sandwich maker and grill till the outside is brown and crisp. Cut and remove the hard sides, and then cut them into three rectangular slices.

For the pulled chicken sandwich, apply butter on both sides of the bread and place separately.

Place the boiled and shredded chicken in a bowl, add mayonnaise, mustard paste, salt, pepper, chopped parsley, and grated cheese. Mix well. Apply this mixture on one slice of bread and cover with another slice. Press gently and cut the hard edges. Cut them in 3 rectangular slices.

Preparation time **10 mins**
Cooking time **15 mins**

Chicken Tenders Serves 2

Chicken tenders are a quick snack. You can bake or fry them. The flavour of oregano and chicken will blow your mind.

8 **chicken strips (boneless)**	1 tsp **oregano**
Salt to taste	Flour for dusting
Pepper to taste	1 **egg**
2 tsp **olive oil**	1 cup **breadcrumbs**
1 tsp **mustard paste**	

Marinate the chicken tenders with salt, pepper, olive oil, thyme, and mustard paste. Add flour with a pinch of salt in a bowl.

In a separate bowl, break the egg with a pinch of salt and beat it. In the third bowl, add breadcrumbs.

Dip the chicken in flour, then egg, and then in breadcrumbs. Place the chicken on a baking tray and place it in a preheated oven to bake at 200°C for 12 to 15 minutes.

Remove and serve hot with ketchup.

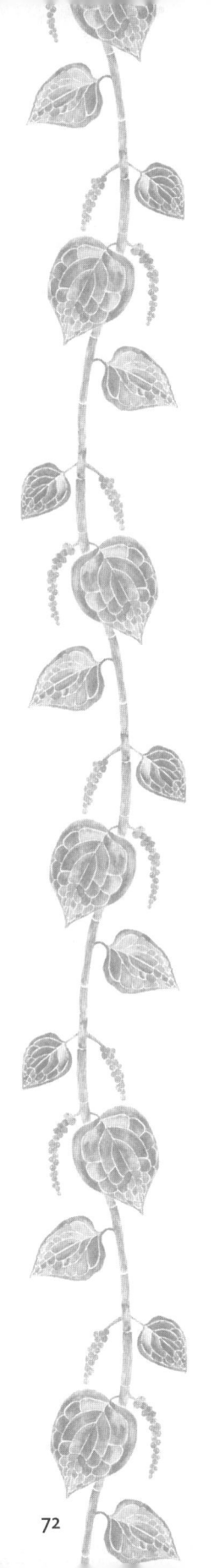

Preparation time **10 mins**
Cooking time **30 mins**

Rosemary Potato Wedges Serves 2

Rosemary goes well with meats as well as potatoes. Baking rosemary with potatoes brings out the flavour of the herb and this dish can be a served as a snack or an accompaniment to grills and roasts.

2 large **potatoes**
Salt to taste
Pepper to taste

A sprig of rosemary
4 garlic cloves
1 tbsp **olive oil**

Wash and clean the potatoes. Do not peel them. Cut them lengthwise into 8 pieces. Sprinkle salt, pepper, and chopped rosemary on them.

Crush garlic with a knife and mix with the potatoes. Drizzle olive oil over them. Preheat the oven to 200°C and bake the potatoes for 30 minutes. Serve hot.

From Top: Granona Parfait (pg 60) French Toast (pg 59)

From Top: Tomatoes and Pickled Beet Salad (pg 62) Baked Mac n' Cheese (pg 64)

From Top: Baked Yoghurt (pg 68), Baked Chicken and Tomato with Potato Mash (pg 63)

From Left: Easy Cupcakes (pg 73), Rosemary Potato Wedges (pg 72), Tomato Bruschetta (pg 69)

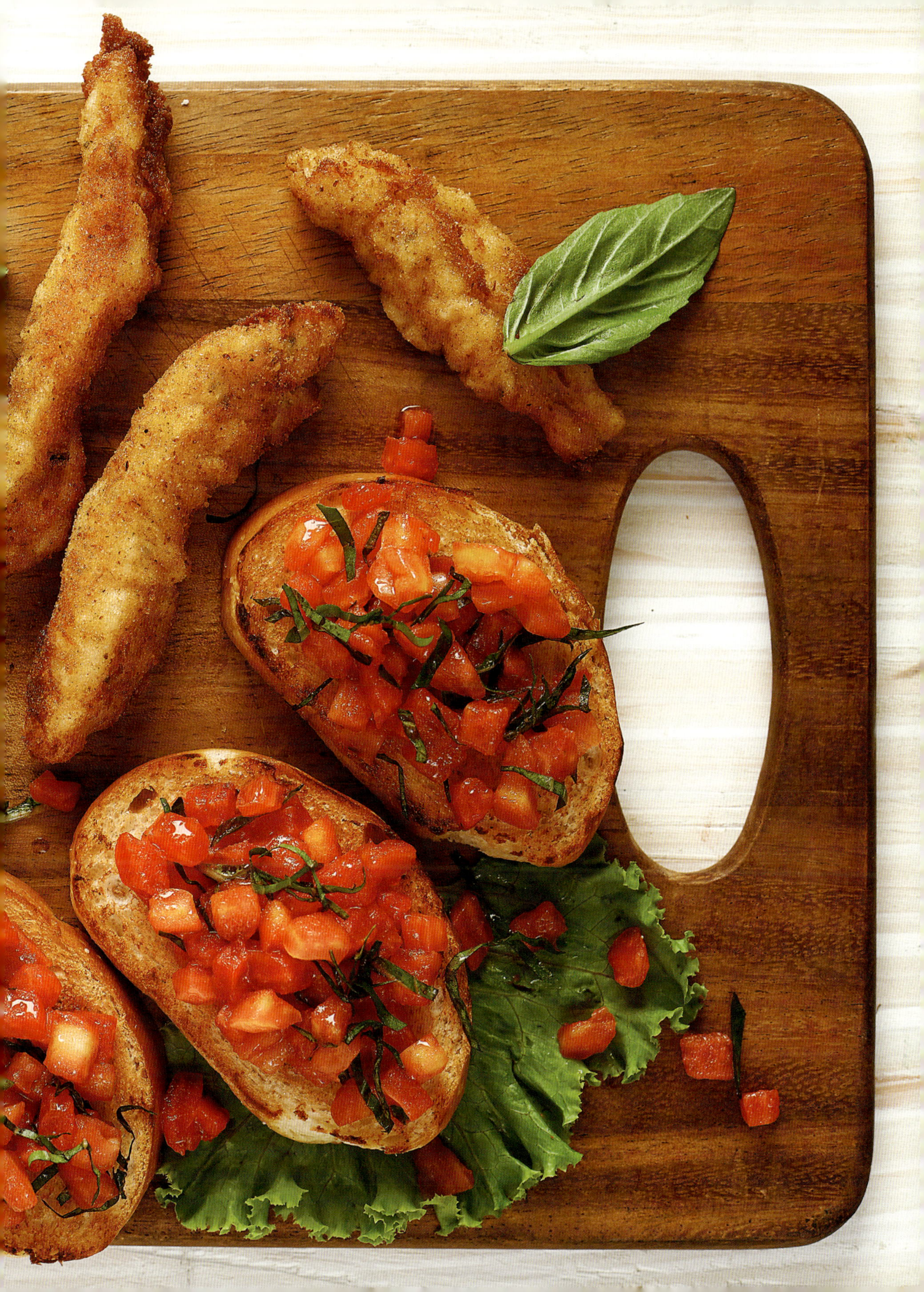

Apple Walnut and Greens (pg 79)

Raw Papaya and Raw Mango Salad (pg 76)

Aubergine, Pomegranate and Garlic Yoghurt Salad (pg 80)

Preparation time 10 mins
Cooking time 15 mins

Easy Cupcakes Serves 8

Party time, valentines, birthdays, anniversary—there's never a dearth of occasions for making and eating cupcakes. Remember the trick is the ratio 1:1:1. Check the quantities below and you will understand.

For Basic Cupcake
100 gm **butter (unsalted)**
100 gm **sugar**
100 gm **flour**
3 **eggs**
1 tsp **vanilla extract**

For Variations
2 tbsp **orange rind**
½ cup **chocolate chips**

For the Icing
1 cup **butter (unsalted)**
2 cups **icing sugar**

Preheat the oven to 180°C. Place the paper cups in the muffin moulds.

Bring the butter to room temperature and add sugar, vanilla extract, and start creaming using a whisk. Keep beating till all the sugar is almost dissolved.

Now add one egg at a time and keep whisking till all the eggs are incorporated and the mixture is light and fluffy.

Sift in the four and gently fold it. Transfer and divide the mixture in paper cases placed in the muffin moulds. Fill only up till three-fourth of the mould as they will rise during baking.

Bake them in the oven at 180°C for 15 minutes. To check, insert a thick needle or knife, if it comes out clean then the cakes are ready.

For a variation in the final batter, mix in the chocolate chips and orange rind and bake as described.

For the icing, cream the butter and slowly add the icing sugar. Once done, place in a piping bag and pipe swirls on the cooled cupcakes.

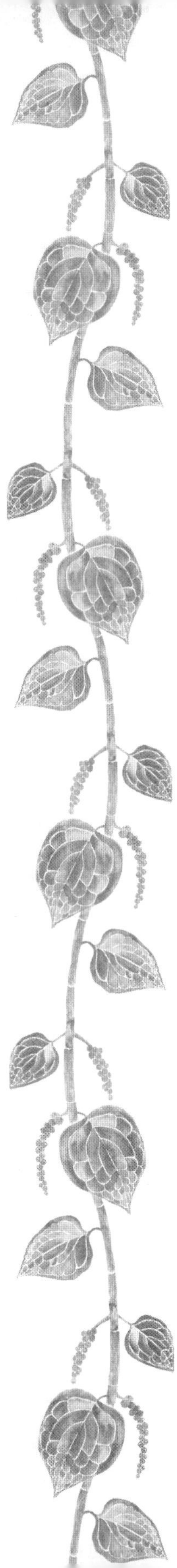

Salads and Soups for the Soul

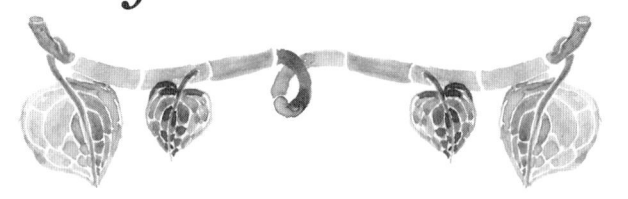

Preparation time **20 mins**

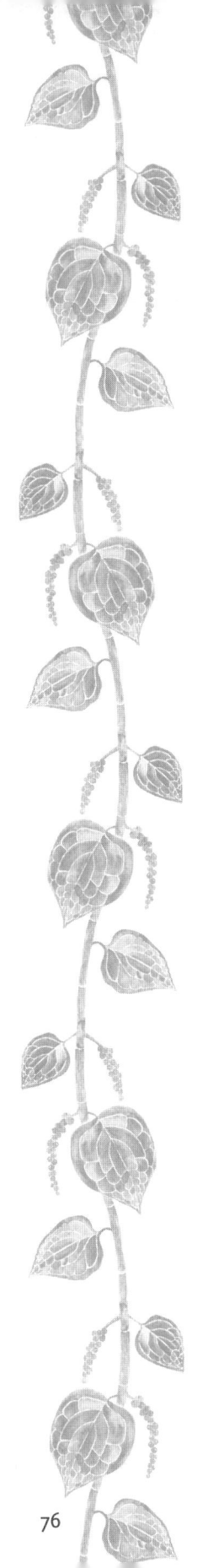

Raw Papaya and Raw Mango Salad Serves 2

This dish is inspired from the popular Thai Som Tam, a raw papaya salad. It is tart and sweet at the same time. The symphony of flavours is well orchestrated in this salad.

3 cups **raw papaya, shredded**
3 cups **raw mango, shredded**
2 cups **French beans, split and crushed**
1 cup **cherry tomatoes, halved**
2 cups **carrot, shredded**
¼ cup **green coriander, chopped**
1 cup **roasted peanuts, crushed**

For the Dressing
3 tbsp **jaggery, grated**
3 **garlic cloves**
1 **red chilli fresh**
5 tbsp **lemon juice**
Salt to taste
2 tbsp **fish sauce**

For the dressing, use a mortar and pestle to smash red chilli and garlic together. Now add fish sauce and lemon juice. Remove.

Using the mortar and pestle, smash the split green beans and place them in a salad bowl. Add the shredded papaya, carrots, raw mango, cherry tomatoes, and peanuts to this.

Pour dressing to the vegetable and toss it nicely. Add salt if required. Garnish with chopped coriander. Serve cold.

Preparation time **20 mins**

Rocket Salad with Stewed Figs and Cheese Serves 2

Don't worry I am not sending you to outer space! Rocket also called arugula is a salad leaf. It has a distinctive pungent and peppery taste and makes a tasty salad. Remember to wash the leaves properly in cold water before using them.

4 big bunches of rocket leaves
2 tbsp olive oil
Salt to taste
Pepper to taste
10 dried figs
A pinch of black salt
¾ cup sugar
¼ cup tamarind pulp
4 tbsp cheese (any cream or soft cheese)

Wash the rocket leaves properly and shake excess water out of them. Place them in the refrigerator to chill.

Boil figs in 2 cups of water. Add tamarind pulp, sugar, and black salt to it. Cook till the tamarind becomes thick and coats the figs. Remove and cool completely.

Place the rocket leaves in a salad bowl and sprinkle salt and pepper. Drizzle olive oil on them. Add the stewed figs and chunks of soft cheese to the salad. Serve cold.

Preparation time **20 mins**

Kimchi: Done My Way Serves 2

Kimchi or Kimchee is the national dish of Korea. It is a fermented salad that has a spicy and sour taste. There are many versions of it and this recipe is how I like it.

6 cups **Chinese cabbage, diced**
3 cups **white raddish, sliced**
2 tbsp **ginger, chopped**
2 tbsp **garlic, chopped**
2 tbsp **chilli powder* (Kashmiri)**
6 tbsp **vinegar**
10 tbsp **sugar**
3 tbsp **fish sauce**
3 cups **spring onions, chopped**
2 tsp **sesame oil**
Salt to taste

In a bowl, place the raddish and cabbage and sprinkle salt generously and mix. Leave aside overnight.

The next morning, wash the cabbage and raddish in cold running water to remove excess salt. Drain all the water properly.

Now place them in a bowl and add ginger, garlic, spring onions, sugar, fish sauce, chilli powder, sesame oil, and vinegar. Mix it well and refrigerate. Serve cold.

*Use a chilli powder that is not hot but gives a bright colour.
The taste of this salad improves with time.

Preparation time **20 mins**

Apple Walnut and Greens Serves 2

Apples and walnuts are a delightful gift from heaven if they are combined together. This is a simple salad to make and is packed with nutrients. The curry powder complements the taste of the apples beautifully.

3 cups **apples, diced**
8 cups **baby lettuce (assorted)**
½ cup **walnuts, toasted**
2 tbsp **olive oil**
4 tbsp **lemon juice**

1 tsp **curry powder**
1 tbsp **honey**
2 tsp **mustard paste**
Salt to taste

In a bowl, place the apples, walnuts, and assorted lettuce.

Separately mix mustard paste, lemon juice, curry powder, honey, and olive oil to make the dressing. Season lightly with salt and pepper.

Pour the dressing over the leaves and apples and serve chilled.

Preparation time 20 mins
Cooking time 15 mins

Aubergine, Pomegranate, and Garlic Yoghurt Salad Serves 2

What more can you ask for after eating this salad with its refreshing Mediterranean flavours? Garlic and pomegranate play the key flavour notes in this salad.

8 baby aubergines
½ tsp turmeric
½ tsp red chilli powder
2 tsp dry mango powder
1 tsp coriander powder
A sprig of basil
2 tbsp olive oil

2 tbsp lemon juice
6 tbsp hung yoghurt
1 garlic, crushed
1 cup pomegranate seeds
2 bunches lettuce
Salt to taste

Slit the aubergines and keep aside. Make a marinade by mixing olive oil, turmeric, red chilli powder, coriander powder, dry mango powder, salt, pepper, and crushed basil leaves.

Marinate the aubergines and place them in a preheated oven at 180°C for 12 to 15 minutes. Remove and allow it to cool.

In another bowl, combine yoghurt with crushed garlic and some salt.

In another bowl, add the lettuce, salt, pepper, and lemon juice. Place the leaves in a salad bowl and drop the aubergines in with dollops of garlic yoghurt.

Sprinkle pomegranate seeds and serve cold.

Preparation time 10 mins
Cooking time 10 mins

Chicken Eggdrop Soup Serves 2

Warm and comforting, this hearty soup of chicken and eggs is perfect for a winter evening. Add lots of vegetables to the soup and you can have it as a complete healthy meal.

750 ml **chicken stock**
2 **eggs**
1 ½ tbsp **soya sauce**
1 tbsp **white vinegar**
1 tbsp **cornflour**

A few drops of **sesame oil**
½ cup **spring onions**, chopped
½ tsp **pepper powder**
Salt to taste

Place the chicken stock in a clean pan and bring to a boil. Now add soya sauce, vinegar, pepper powder, and salt.

Mix in 4 tbsp of water into the cornflour and pour this slowly into the soup to thicken it.

Whisk the eggs and pour it into the soup in a steady stream, continuously stirring the soup so that it doesn't form lumps.

Remove from heat and add spring onions and sesame oil. Serve hot.

Preparation time 10 mins
Cooking time 25 mins

Bhuttae ka Shorba with Chilli Butter Popcorns (Indian Corn Soup) Serves 4

India is famous for serving spicy roasted corn on the cob. This version is a take on the corn on the cob but the spices evoke the similar taste of street side masala corn.

3 cups sweet corn kernels
3 tbsp oil
2 tsp jeera
1 bay leaf
½ cup onions, chopped
2 tbsp ginger, chopped
2 tbsp, garlic, chopped
1 green chilli, slit
2 tbsp refined flour

1 tsp salt
½ tsp black pepper powder
1 tsp chaat masala
½ cup green coriander

For Chilli Butter Popcorns
1 cup popcorn
1 tbsp butter
A pinch of chilli powder

Make a purée of sweet corn and keep aside. In a pan, heat oil, add bay leaf, and jeera. Now add the finely chopped onions, green chilli, ginger, and garlic.

Lower the heat and cook till the onions are transparent. Add the refined flour and sauté till blonde in colour. Now add the sweet corn mash and sauté for 3 to 5 minutes. Add sufficient water and give it a quick boil and then simmer for 5 to 7 minutes.

Adjust seasoning and finally mix in the chopped coriander and sprinkle chaat masala over it.

Melt butter and pour over the popcorn, sprinkle red chilli powder, and serve along with the soup.

Preparation time 15 mins
Cooking time 20 mins

Kaddu ka Shorba (Pumpkin Soup) Serves 4

Pumpkin is my personal favourite as it is one of the most versatile vegetables. This recipe makes a velvety soup that has light keynotes of the natural sweetness of pumpkin. And spiked with butter and fennel seeds it is simply divine.

4 cups **pumpkin**, diced
1 cup **potatoes**, diced
3 tbsp **butter**
1 **bay leaf**
1 tbsp **fennel seeds**
5 **peppercorns**
A pinch of **nutmeg**
A sprig of **sage**

1 cup **onion**, diced
1 cup **carrots**, diced
1 tbsp **garlic**, crushed
Salt to taste
100 ml **cream**
2 litres **water or vegetable stock**
Dill leaves for garnishing (optional)

Melt butter in a thick-bottomed pan. Add bay leaf, peppercorns, and fennel seeds. When they start to crackle, add the onions, carrots, sage, garlic, potatoes, and pumpkin. Sauté for 3 minutes on a low flame.

Add salt and water or vegetable stock to this. Allow a quick boil and then gently simmer for 8 minutes.

Remove from fire and strain (do not throw the stock away). Now, make a purée of these vegetables and add it back to the stock.

Bring to a boil and add the cream. Add a pinch of nutmeg and chopped dill. Serve hot.

Preparation time **15 mins**
Cooking time **20 mins**

Minestroni Serves 4

Minestroni soup has a base of tomatoes and can be made with seasonal vegetables. The best way to enjoy this hearty soup is to make it fresh in the morning and enjoy it through the day. The Italian Mafia once swore by this wholesome soup!

3 tbsp **olive oil**
1 **bay leaf**
½ cup **onion, chopped**
2 tbsp **garlic, chopped**
½ cup **celery, chopped**
A **sprig of oregano**
½ cup of **carrots, chopped**
1 cup **zucchini, chopped**
1 cup **white kidney beans, boiled**
½ cup **potatoes, diced**
2 ½ cups **tomatoes, chopped** (without skin and seeds)
1 cup **macaroni**
2 **sprigs of basil**
Salt to taste
Pepper powder to taste
½ cup **Parmesan or any hard cheese** (optional)
1 litre **vegetable stock or water**

In a thick-bottomed pan, add olive oil and bay leaf. Now add chopped onions, oregano, garlic, and celery. Sauté for a minute and add carrots, zucchini, and potatoes. Sauté for 2 minutes on medium flame.

Now add the beans and tomatoes and cook for 3 minutes.

Add about 1 litre of vegetable stock and bring it to a boil. Add macaroni and keep it on simmer till it gets cooked.

Season with salt and pepper and add basil. Cook till the soup gets a little body. Transfer into serving dishes and garnish with shaved Parmesan cheese or any hard cheese.

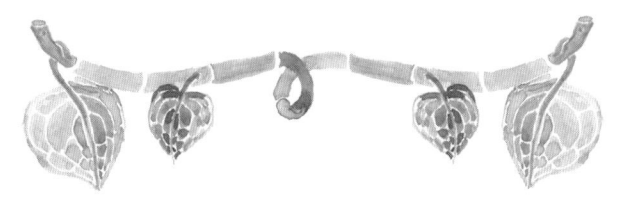

Breads and Rice

Preparation time **15 mins**
Cooking time **10 mins**

Tortilla (Mexican flat bread) Makes 12 pieces

Tortilla is hugely popular in Mexico and the States. Around the world, Mexican restaurants use this versatile bread to serve with a variety of foods. It can be made using regular flour or cornmeal flour. Easy to make, this bread has multiple uses in the culinary world.

2 cups **refined flour**
1 tsp **salt**
1 tsp **baking powder**
1 ½ tbsp **butter**
1 cup **water**

Mix flour, salt, baking powder, and butter together and knead well.

Add cold water and knead till it turns into an elastic, soft dough. Let it rest for 5 minutes, and then divide this into equal-sized balls.

Use a rolling pin to flatten the balls into a thin and round shape.

Heat a tawa or pan and cook them on both sides like a roti. Cook till it is three-fourths done on both sides and put them aside. Cover them with a clean kitchen cloth to keep them moist.

Preparation time **20 mins**
Cooking time **10 mins**

Khoye ka Parantha Serves 4

Semi sweet milk solids stuffed in a wholewheat bread is a common sight in the streets of Old Delhi, India. Paranthae wali galli (in Old Delhi), which literally means 'Bread Street', is legendary for this stuffed bread. If you can't make it there, go ahead and make it yourself in the comfort of your own home!

400 gm **wheat flour**
Water as required
½ tsp **salt**
2 tbsp **ghee (clarified butter)**

For the Stuffing
120 gm **khoya**
½ tsp **turmeric**

½ tsp **red chilli powder**
2 tsp **coriander, cracked**
2 tsp **green chilli, chopped**
2 tsp **ginger, chopped**
½ tsp **salt**
1 tbsp **coriander, chopped**

Keep aside around 50 gm of flour for rolling out the dough. In the remaining flour, add salt and water and make a soft dough. Let it rest.

For the stuffing, mix khoya, turmeric, red chilli, cracked coriander, coriander, green chilli, ginger, and salt.

Now divide the dough equally and shape it into balls. Take a spoonful of stuffing and press it into the dough and seal it. Now roll them out flat using dry flour and give it a flat, round shape.

Heat a flat tawa and cook the parantha on both sides. Apply ghee and make it nice and crisp. Serve hot with yoghurt.

Preparation time 15 mins
Cooking time 10 mins

Khoba Roti Serves 4

Khoba, which means incisions on bread, makes this Rajasthani bread a delightful sight. It is so pretty that it is the single most reason to go ahead and try it. These incisions help to capture the extra ghee or butter in which it is cooked. I have added a few of my own flavours to enhance the taste.

2 ½ cups **whole wheat flour**
Salt to taste
2 tsp **ajwain**

1 tbsp **fenugreek leaves**
½ cup **ghee, clarified butter**

Mix together flour, salt, 1 tbsp ghee, ajwain, fenugreek leaves, and water to make a stiff dough. Let it rest for 10 minutes.

Now divide the dough into balls. Roll out round and thick discs about 8"diameter. Using your fingers, push, pinch and lift the dough at various places to make indents and pinches on the surface. Do the same on the sides as well.

Heat a griddle and cook with the pinched side up first, then turn. Apply ghee on both sides and cook on medium heat for a nicely done crisp bread. Serve hot.

Bhutte ka Shorba with Chilli Butter Popcorn (pg 82)

Minestroni (pg 84)

Chicken Machboos (pg 94)

Khoba Roti (pg 88)

Khoye ka Parantha (pg 87)

Olive Parantha (pg 89)

Preparation time 10 mins
Cooking time 10 mins

Olive Parantha Serves 6

When I worked in the Gulf I was introduced to so many varieties of olives and olive oils that it inspired me to create my own olive bread. You can cook this bread in an oven or on a hot griddle. Use it as an accompaniment or eat it with a dip.

2 ½ cups wheat flour
Salt to taste
1 tbsp sesame seeds
2 tsp Nigella seeds
1 green chilli, chopped
2 tbsp olive oil

1 cup olives, chopped
2 sprigs of basil leaves, chopped
2 tbsp dill leaves, chopped
1 tbsp garlic, chopped
½ tsp baking powder

To make the parantha, mix all the ingredients in wheat flour and half the olive oil. Add water to make the dough soft. Let it rest for 10 minutes.

Now roll out the parantha, make a cut from the centre towards the outer edge of the parantha. Drizzle a little oil and start rolling the parantha from the open end to make a cone. Let it rest for another 10 minutes.

Now press the cone and roll out into a round parantha. On a hot tawa, cook on both sides till brown. Apply olive oil to the hot parantha and serve.

Preparation time **15 mins**
Cooking time **10 mins**

Roti Jala 12 pieces

On a culinary trip to South East Asia, I discovered a beautiful bread which had the texture and design straight from the architecture of the maharajas of India. This is a perfect accompaniment for curries and stews and is fun to make.

2 ½ cups **refined flour**	**Water** as required
1 tsp **salt**	1 **egg** (country egg)
150 ml **coconut cream**	2 tbsp **ghee**, clarified butter

Combine all the ingredients except ghee and make it into a smooth and runny batter, slightly thinner than pancake batter.

Heat a pan and pour the batter in a roti jala mould. Alternatively pour the batter into a bottle with a thin nozzle.

Pipe out thin streams of batter in the form of lacy patterns starting from the outside to the inside. Drizzle some ghee and cook on both sides. Serve hot with curry.

Preparation time 35 mins
Cooking time 10 mins

Pita Bread Serves 10

Pita is a popular bread in the Middle Eastern and Mediterranean regions. It has several variations. This one is a basic version and is easy to make. Once baked, place under a damp cloth so that it does not dry up.

3 cups **refined flour**
1 tsp **salt**
2 tsp **dry yeast**

2 tsp **sugar**
2 tbsp **olive oil**
1 cup **approximately water**

In lukewarm water, add sugar, yeast, and 2 tbsp of flour. Allow it to sit until the water becomes frothy.

Now separately mix salt and flour and knead the dough using the frothy water. Make it into a soft dough and knead it for another 5 minutes.

Apply oil and allow it to rest till it becomes double its size. Now divide the dough into equal-sized balls and roll it out into a round shape, about 6" and 2 mm thick.

Heat the oven to 180°C and place the pita and cook till the bread puffs up. Wait for another minute and then remove. Stack the bread one top of the other and serve.

Preparation time **15 mins**
Cooking time **10 mins**

Stir Fried Rice Serve 2 cups

This is the best way to make Chinese style rice. Eat it on its own or with meat or vegetables.

2 cups **rice, boiled**
2 ½ tbsp **oil**
2 tsp **garlic, chopped**
2 tsp **ginger, chopped**
2 tbsp **onion, chopped**
2 tbsp **carrots, chopped**

2 tbsp **French beans, finely chopped**
Salt to taste
Black pepper powder to taste
2 tsp **soya sauce**
4 tbsp **spring onions, chopped**

Make sure the boiled rice is cooled and at room temperature when you set out to cook.

Heat oil in a wok/kadai/deep pan and add chopped garlic and ginger. Sauté for 30 seconds and add onions, carrots, and beans. Sauté for a minute and add the boiled rice.

Toss well and then add salt, pepper, and soya sauce. Toss again for 2 minutes and then throw in the spring onions and toss again and serve hot.

Preparation time 15 mins
Cooking time 10 mins

Yakhni Pulao Serve 4

Yakhni pulao is made using the stock of mutton/lamb. It is a meal on its own and can be had with a light curry or yoghurt.

1 ½ cups **Basmati rice**
3 cups **mutton stock**
1/3 cup **oil**
1 **bay leaf**
1 **black cardamom**
2 **cloves**
5 **peppercorns**

1 tsp **fennel seeds**
1 ½ cup **onion, sliced**
2 tbsp **garlic, chopped**
1 tbsp **ginger, chopped**
1 cup **yoghurt**
Salt to taste

Wash and soak the rice in water for 45 minutes. Heat oil in a pan and add bay leaf, black cardamom, cloves, peppercorn, and fennel seeds. Sauté for a minute. Now add the sliced onions.

Whisk the yoghurt and keep aside. Brown the onions. Remove one-fourth of the browned onions and reserve for garnishing. Immediately add chopped garlic and ginger in the same oil; sauté but do not brown. Quickly add yoghurt and turn on to high flame.

Keep stirring till the yoghurt comes to a boil. Now add the stock and salt and give it another boil. Drain the rice and add to the stock.

Cook covered till the rice absorbs all the liquid and gets cooked. Serve garnished with brown onions.

Preparation time 15 mins
Cooking time 40 mins

Chicken Machboos Serves 4

Machboos or Kabsa is a famous Middle Eastern rice dish. Almost every nook and corner in the Arabic world will serve this dish with pride.

For the Chicken
1 whole chicken (skin on)
1 tbsp coriander powder
2 tsp cumin powder
½ tsp turmeric
2 tbsp lemon juice
½ cup yoghurt
1 tsp red chilli powder
1 tbsp olive oil
1 tbsp tomato paste
Salt to taste

For the Rice
2 cups Basmati rice
½ cup olive oil
1 tbsp butter
A few strands of saffron
2 cups onions, sliced
¼ cup raisins
¼ cup cashewnuts
¼ cup almonds
1 cup mint leaves
4 cups chicken stock (optional)
½ cup parsley or coriander, chopped

Soak the rice for half an hour in water. Soak saffron in 2 tbsp of warm water.

Cut the chicken in four (2 legs, 2 breast). Pat dry the chicken. Apply salt and lemon juice on it and keep aside for 10 minutes. Now mix all the remaining ingredients and rub into the chicken.

Roast the chicken in a pre-heated oven at 180°C for 30 minutes. In a separate pan, heat oil and add sliced onions and brown them. Remove and keep aside. In the same oil, add the dry fruits and on a low heat lightly toast them.

Remove and keep aside. In the same oil, add the butter and as soon as it melts, add mint leaves and immediately add chicken stock or water. Give it a boil and add the drained rice. Add salt and cook. Once the rice is three-fourths done pour the dissolved saffron over the rice. Do not stir. Allow the rice to absorb all the water.

Once the rice is done take it out on a platter, sprinkle with fried nuts and brown onions and place the roasted chicken on top. Sprinkle coriander leaves and serve.

Preparation time 15 mins
Cooking time 10 mins

Tawa Pulao Serves 4

Tawa is the Indian iron griddle and it has several uses. From preparing starters to main courses, from making rice and breads to desserts, this is a versatile kitchen equipment. Tawa Pulao means rice prepared on a flat iron griddle.

4 cups **Basmati rice, boiled**
¼ cup **oil**
1 tbsp **cumin**
1 tbsp **garlic, chopped**
1 tbsp **ginger, chopped**
¾ cup **onion, chopped**
1 **green chilli, chopped**
½ tsp **turmeric**
1 tsp **red chilli powder**
2 tsp **coriander powder**
Salt to taste
1 cup **tomatoes, chopped**
½ cup **capsicum, chopped**
1 cup **mint leaves**
1 cup **browned onions**

In a pan, pour oil and add cumin. When it starts to crackle, add garlic, ginger, and green chilli. Sauté for a minute and add onions, sauté till transparent. Now add the capsicum and sauté for another minute.

Add turmeric, red chilli powder, and coriander powder. Sauté and add 2 tbsp of water so that the spices don't burn. Now add the tomatoes and sauté till they wilt.

Now add boiled Basmati rice and mix with flat spatulas. At this time, add salt, mint leaves, and browned onions. Serve hot.

Hearty Main Courses

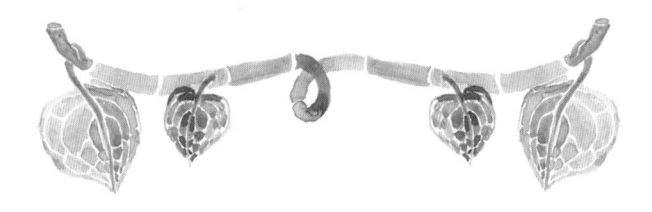

Preparation time **10 mins**
Cooking time **15 mins**

Charmoula Rubbed Grilled Fish Serves 2

Charmoula is a rub or marinade that goes very well with seafood. It is commonly found in the cuisines of Algeria, Tunisia, and Morocco. A brilliant combination of coriander, spices, and olive oil, which has a very subtle yet expressive flavour.

600 gm whole fish (cleaned and gutted)	Pepper powder to taste
5 tbsp charmoula*	**1 tbsp** lemon juice
Salt to taste	Lemon wedges for garnishing

Pat dry the cleaned and gutted fish. Using a sharp knife, make small slits on the flesh of the fish on both sides, from top to bottom. Apply lemon juice and sprinkle salt and pepper. Keep aside for 10 minutes.

Rub the charmoula on the fish and leave aside for 10 minutes. Preheat an oven to 170°C, and bake the fish for approximately 25 minutes.

*For the charmoula recipe see p 49.
The time required to cook the fish depends upon the thickness of the fish.

Preparation time 10 mins
Cooking time 20 mins

Prawns Moilee Serves 2

This very popular dish from the coastal state of Kerela, India, is unique because of the subtle flavours of coconut and curry leaves sauce. Moilee sauce is now fancied the world over with big restaurants now serving it in different ways. You can add almost any vegetable or meat to this sauce and it will turn out delicious. Here's something you can't go wrong with.

- 12 prawns (medium size)
- 2 tbsp coconut oil
- 1 tsp fenugreek
- 2 tsp mustard seeds
- 2 dried red chillies
- 2 sprigs of curry leaves
- 1 cup onion, sliced
- 2 tbsp ginger chopped
- 2 tbsp garlic, chopped
- 1 green chilli, slit
- 1 ½ cup tomatoes, diced
- 1 tsp turmeric
- 1 tbsp tamarind
- ½ tsp black pepper powder
- Salt to taste

Heat coconut oil in a pan and add fenugreek seeds, mustard seeds, and dried red chillies. When they start to crackle, add curry leaves, sliced onions, green chilli, ginger, and garlic. Sauté till it starts to brown.

Now add turmeric and sauté over a low heat. Add tomato dices and sauté.

Mix 1 cup of water to the coconut milk and pour it in the pan. Cook the curry on a low heat and after 5 minutes, toss in the prawns and pepper powder.

Once the prawns are cooked add the tamarind paste. Check for seasoning again and serve hot with steamed rice or roti jala.

Preparation time **10 mins**
Cooking time **20 mins**

Steamed Fish with Ginger and Light Soy *Serves 2*

Best way to enjoy Asian style seafood is when it is cooked in a bamboo steamer. Steaming preserves the flavour of the fish while the ginger and soy seep into the fish to make it really flavourful. Light and easy, this dish is best served with rice.

400 gm **fish fillet** (2 pieces)	2 tbsp **light soya sauce**
½ cup **ginger juliennes**	2 tsp **sesame oil**
1 **fresh red chilli**, chopped	2 tsp **sugar**
1 cup **spring onion juliennes**	1 ½ tbsp **lemon juice**
3 tbsp **oil**	**Pepper powder** to taste
7 to 8 sprigs **of coriander**	**Salt** to taste

Pat dry the fish and place it on a plate. Sprinkle salt and pepper, and arrange half of the ginger juliennes on top of it.

Prepare a steamer and place the fish in it and cook it for 15 minutes or till it is done.

Remove the fish and arrange the rest of the ginger, coriander sprigs, red chilli, and spring onions on top of the fish. Heat oil till it is quite hot and using a spoon, pour the oil over the fish.

Combine sesame oil, soy sauce, sugar, and lemon juice and pour over the fish. Serve immediately.

Preparation time 10 mins (requires 5 hrs of marination)
Cooking time 20 mins

Char Siu Mutton Chops Serves 2

In the early days, cooking was a simple business. One of the ways of cooking meat was to fork up strips of meat and roast it in an oven. Char Sui literally translated means 'Fork Roast'. This dish is authentically prepared with pork, but lamb and chicken also work very well. The outside of the meat is sticky sweet and has a light flavour of the five spice powder.

10 **mutton chops (double boned)**
1 cup **char siu sauce***
1 tbsp **sugar**
2 tsp **honey**

2 tsp **five spice powder****
½ cup **spring onions, chopped**
½ cup **ginger, chopped**

Clean the chops and pat dry. In a bowl, add the char siu sauce, sugar, honey, five spice powder, spring onions, and ginger. Keep it aside for 4 to 5 hours or overnight in the refrigerator.

Once marinated, heat your oven to 180°C and let the meat cook for about 20 minutes or till done. Serve with Chinese fried rice.

* Char Siu sauce is available at most Asian stores.
**You can buy a readymade five spice recipe from a store.

Preparation time **15 mins**
Cooking time **35 mins**

Sheppard's Pie Serves 2

An iconic British dish, Sheppard's Pie goes perfectly with a winter evening. This is hearty and robust soul food at its best and a complete meal in itself.

300 gm **mutton mince**
3 cups **potato mash***
1 **egg yolk**
½ cup **olive oil**
1 **bay leaf**
¾ cup **onions**, chopped

A sprig of **thyme**
2 tbsp **flour**
1 ½ tbsp **Worcestershire sauce**
1 cup **tomato purée**
Salt to taste
Pepper to taste

Heat oil in a pan and add the bay leaf and chopped onions. Sauté and add thyme, and then add flour and sauté for a minute. Now add the mince and cook on a high flame to brown the meat.

Add Worcestershire sauce, salt, and pepper. Sauté and then add the tomato purée. Cook for 3 to 4 minutes. Add 2 cups of water and cook till water evaporates.

Separately add an egg yolk to the mash and keep aside. In an oven proof dish, place the mince and on top smear a thick layer of potato mash and bake in an oven at 180°C till the potatoes get a good brown colour.

*For the recipe of potato mash see p 67.

Preparation time **15 mins**
Cooking time **35 mins**

Goulash Serves 2

I learnt this goulash recipe from Chef Thomas, the Executive Chef of Leela Kempinski, Gurgaon, India. He is Austrian by birth but has lived all over the world. He is passionate about cooking and respects the authenticity of cuisines. I was surprised when he told me that Roganjosh, Indian lamb curry, is almost the same as Hungarian goulash. This prompted me to ask him to cook the goulash for me. And boy, was it good!

400 gm **mutton cubes (1"x1")**
½ cup **oil**
2 tsp **caraway seeds**
1 **bay leaf**
A **sprig of rosemary**
2 cups **onions, chopped**
2 tbsp **garlic, chopped**
Salt to taste
1 ½ tbsp **paprika powder***
4 cups **tomato purée (fresh)**
2 cups **stock or water**

Place the fresh tomato purée in a pan and give it a quick boil. Lower heat and keep simmering to reduce it till half.

Heat oil in a pan and add bay leaf, caraway seeds, chopped onions, rosemary, and garlic. Sauté for 2 to 3 minutes. Now add the mutton cubes and cook on high heat to brown them. This will take a while.

Now add paprika powder and cook for another minute.

Add salt and then the reduced tomato purée. Cook for 5 minutes and then add 2 cups water and boil until meat is tender.

Serve hot with bread or rice.

*You can use deggi mirch or any mild/sweet chilli powder instead of paprika.

Preparation time **10 mins**
Cooking time **25 mins**

Lamb Skewers with Yoghurt Dip Serves 2

Tiny lamb or mutton cubes on small skewers works best for an evening garden party. Dill and yoghurt complement the flavours of the lamb excellently when it is cooked on an open fire.

400 gm **lamb/mutton cubes**
1 cup **onion paste**
2 tbsp **garlic paste**
2 tbsp **ginger paste**
3 tbsp **lemon juice**
1 tbsp **raw papaya paste**
1 tbsp **green chilli paste**
2 tsp **coriander powder**
2 tsp **cumin powder**

Salt to taste
Oil for basting

For the Dip
1 cup **hung yoghurt**
2 tsp **garlic paste**
Salt to taste
1 tbsp **dill, chopped**
¼ tsp **black pepper powder**

Pat dry the mutton and rub the raw papaya paste on it. Now apply salt, lemon juice, ginger, garlic, and green chilli paste. Leave for 10 minutes. Now apply onion paste, coriander powder, and cumin powder.

Keep the mutton in this marinade for at least 2 hours. Now skewer the lamb cubes on wooden or metal skewers and cook on an open flame or alternatively cook them in a preheated oven at 180°C for 20 minutes or till it is cooked.

In between, baste with oil to keep it moist.

For the dip, combine all the ingredients and serve with the hot skewers.

Lamb Skewers with Yoghurt Dip (pg 104)

Sheppard's Pie (pg 102)

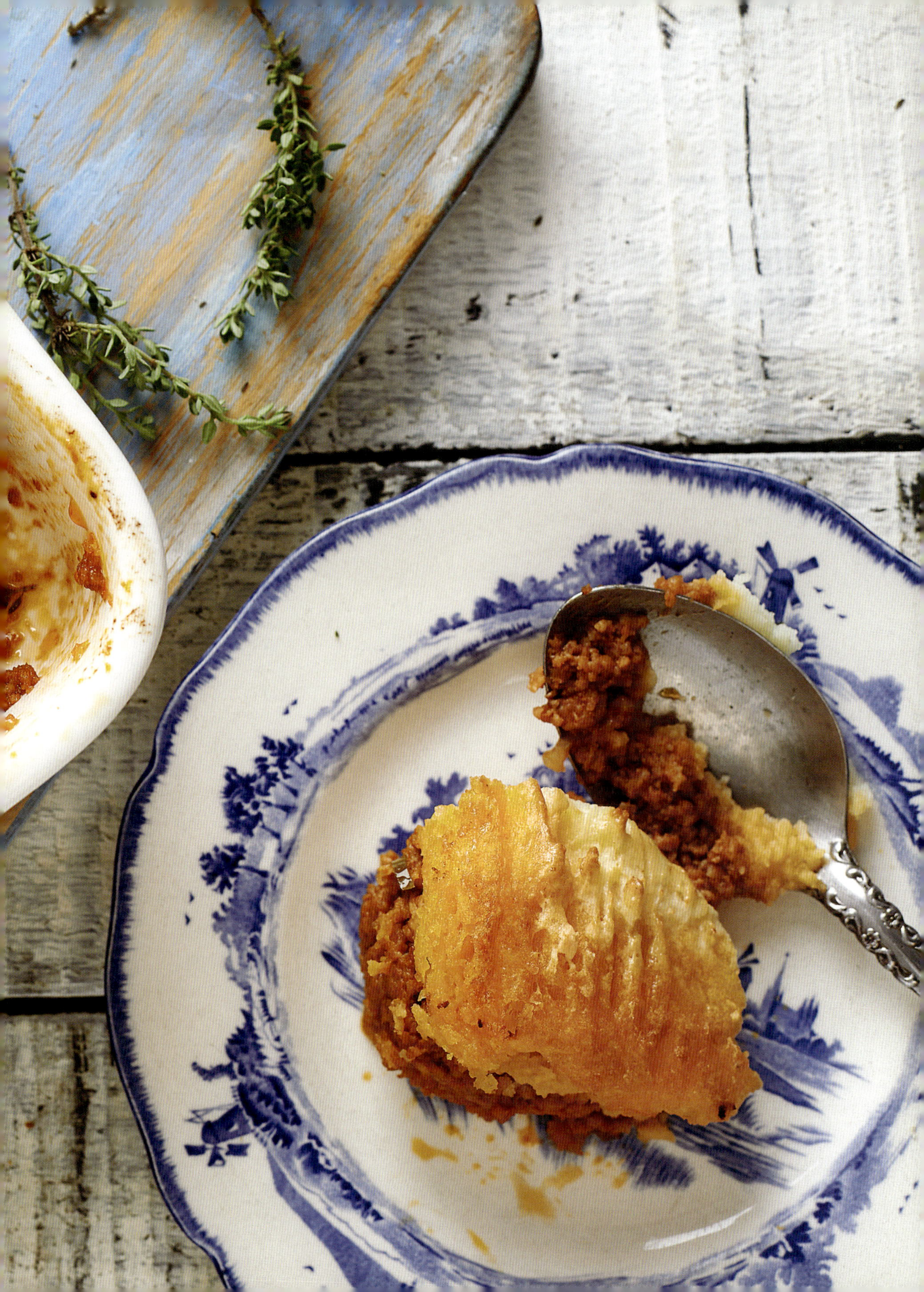

Soy Marinated Chicken with Chilli Coriander (pg 105)

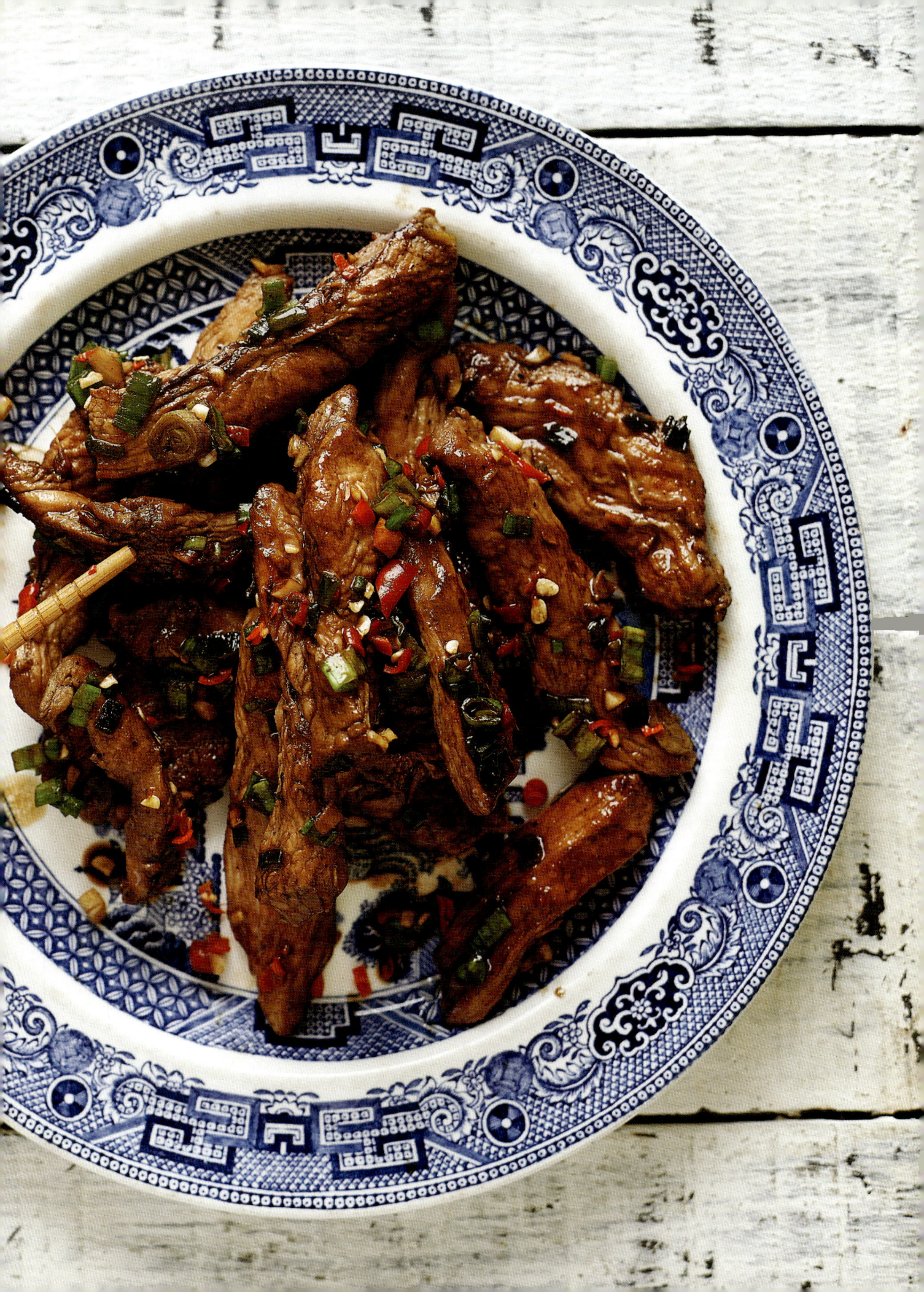

Charmoula Rubbed Grilled Fish (pg 98)

Filipino Chicken Adobo (pg 107)

Hainese Chicken Rice (pg 110)

Preparation time **15 mins**
Cooking time **10 mins**

Soy Marinated Chicken with Chilli Coriander Serves 2

Soya sauce lends its distinct umami taste to the chicken in this recipe. This is the quickest chicken dish I know and it is packed with flavour. The soya sauce gives deep, savoury, earthy flavours to the chicken and the ginger and chilli take care of the rest. Enjoy this with a heap of boiled rice.

400 gm **chicken (boneless)**
1 tbsp **ginger, chopped**
1 tbsp **garlic, chopped**
Crushed black pepper to taste
1 tbsp **Chinese rice wine or vinegar**
½ cup **light soya sauce**
2 tbsp **oyster sauce**
¼ cup **spring onion**
1 tsp **sugar**
1 **fresh red chilli, chopped**
1 ½ tbsp **butter**
2 tbsp **fresh coriander**

Cut the chicken into thin strips of 1 cm thickness. Marinate the chicken in all the ingredients except butter and coriander. Keep this aside for 10 minutes.

Melt butter in a pan and add the chicken. Cook on a medium heat till the chicken is done.

Transfer the chicken to a platter and garnish with fresh coriander. Serve with rice.

Preparation time **10 mins**
Cooking time **10 mins**

Chicken Schnitzel Serves 2

Schnitzel is a German dish which is always made with veal, but my recipe uses chicken and it comes out equally beautiful and tasty. The look of a freshly-fried schnitzel is an invitation to binge.

4 chicken breasts	2 cups flour
Black pepper powder to taste	3 eggs
A sprig of thyme	2 cups breadcrumbs
1 tbsp mustard paste (Dijon)	2 lemon wedges
Oil for frying	Salt to taste

Pat dry the chicken breast. Lightly beat it with the back of the knife at places where it is plump to flatten it out.

Sprinkle salt, thyme, and pepper over it and then rub mustard paste over it.

Break eggs in a bowl and add a little salt and whisk them. Now coat the breast in flour, pat it, and then dip it in the whisked eggs. Give the chicken a good coating of breadcrumbs. Try and coat them evenly.

Heat oil and deep fry the breast till golden brown. Serve with a lemon wedge.

Preparation time **10 mins**
Cooking time **20 mins**

Filipino Chicken Adobo Serves 2

This recipe was first served to me by a hostess in my restaurant in Kuwait. Hard to believe that the simple dish tasted fantastic and required only few basic ingredients. Once you have cooked this dish you will realize that you can cook almost any world cuisine in your kitchen.

6 chicken drumsticks
6 tbsp **soya sauce**
Pepper powder to taste
1 ½ cup **onion, sliced**

3 tbsp **garlic, sliced**
2 tbsp **vinegar**
2 tbsp **oil**

Marinate the chicken in all the ingredients and keep it aside for 10 minutes.

Heat a pan and place the chicken. Cover and cook on a low flame. Add 1 cup water and cook till the chicken is done. Serve with steamed rice.

Preparation time **10 mins**
Cooking time **20 mins**

Chicken Cacciatora Serves 2

Cacciatora means 'hunter' in Italian. This dish is originally made with rabbit but chicken works just fine too. A simple, rustic, hearty, and meaty dish. Simply Italiano!

500 gm **chicken (on the bone)**
4 tbsp **olive oil**
1 **bay leaf**
A **sprig of rosemary**
½ cup **onions, chopped**
2 tbsp **garlic, chopped**
¼ cup **carrots, chopped**
¼ cup **celery, chopped**
¼ cup **mushrooms, chopped**
8 **tomatoes**
¾ cup **white wine**
¼ cup **parsley, chopped**
Salt to taste
Pepper powder to taste

Make small crisscross cuts on the tomatoes. Blanch the tomatoes for 10 seconds in hot water and immediately dip them in cold water. Remove the skin and seeds and dice the tomatoes.

Sprinkle salt and pepper over the chicken. Heat oil, add the chicken and brown them from the outside and remove.

In the same oil, add bay leaf, rosemary, onions, garlic, carrots, mushrooms, and celery. Sauté them till they turn a bit brown. Add wine and allow it to evaporate. Now add the chicken and tomatoes back into this. Sauté and add some water if required.

Cook till the chicken is done. Garnish with parsley and serve hot.

Preparation time 10 mins
Cooking time 20 mins

Chicken and Potato Stew Serves 2

I have been fortunate to train at Karavali—the award-winning South Indian restaurant at Taj Gateway Hotel, Bangalore. It serves the best coastal cuisine in India. Growing up in Delhi, my knowledge of South Indian was limited to masala dosas and idli sambhars. I had been a fool for the longest time. Everything changed for me the day I started working at this restaurant. I became much wiser to begin with!

400 gm chicken (on the bone)
4 tbsp coconut oil
2 dried red chillies
1 tbsp Mustard seeds
2 sprigs curry leaves
½ cup ginger julienne
¼ cup garlic, sliced
1 cup onion, sliced
1 green chill, slit
1 tsp turmeric
1 tsp red chilli powder
1 tbsp Madras curry powder
12 baby potatoes (peeled)
Salt to taste
2 ½ cups coconut milk (thick)
2 tbsp tamarind pulp

Heat coconut oil and add mustard seeds and dried red chillies. When it crackles, add curry leaves, sliced onions, green chillies, ginger, and garlic. Sauté till the onions turn transparent.

Now add turmeric, red chilli powder, and Madras curry powder. Add ½ cup water and cook the spices. Add the potatoes and salt. Sauté for 3 minutes and now add the chicken.

Cook till chicken is half done. Now add coconut milk mixed with 1 ½ cups of water. Cover and cook on low heat till the chicken and potatoes are done. Add tamarind pulp to the curry to adjust the acidity.

Preparation time 15 mins
Cooking time 60 mins

Hainese Chicken Rice Serves 4

My first bite of this dish was in Singapore. My flight was at an odd time and by the time I landed I was starved and all I could think of was food. I stopped the car on the way to the hotel and dashed into a small family take-out shop. I ordered the chicken rice without thinking. I presumed it would be a chicken curry and rice, but what arrived was plain rice topped with boiled chicken. Famished, I dug into the rice and was left speechless. I polished the dish off in no time and couldn't thank the family enough for a meal. You will fall in love with this dish.

For the Chicken
1 kg chicken (whole, skin on)
Salt to taste
½ cup ginger, sliced
6 cloves garlic, smashed
2 spring onion stalks
2 tsp sesame oil
1 tbsp light soya sauce

For the Rice
2 ½ cups rice
½ cup ginger, chopped
½ cup garlic, chopped
2 tsp sesame oil
2 tbsp oil
2 ½ cups chicken stock*
Salt to taste

For the Chilli Sauce
2 fresh red chillies fresh, chopped
2 tsp sugar
2 tsp ginger, chopped
2 tsp garlic, chopped
2 tbsp lemon juice
1 tbsp light soya sauce
¾ cup chicken stock*

For Garnishing
4 sprigs of coriander
½ cup spring onion, chopped
1 tbsp red chilli juliennes

Wash and soak the rice for half an hour. Pat dry the chicken. Rub salt, sesame oil, and light soya sauce evenly inside and outside and under the skin. Now fill the cavity of the chicken with ginger, garlic, and spring onions.

Fill water in a pan and place the chicken. The water level should be enough to cover the chicken. Now gently boil the chicken for 40 minutes on low heat. Remove scum as and when it appears.

Remove the chicken and strain the stock. This chicken stock will be required to prepare rice and the chilli sauce.

In another pan, heat oil, add ginger and garlic. Sauté but do not brown them. Add rice and 5 cups of chicken stock. Add salt and sesame oil. Cook the rice till all the liquid is absorbed and the rice is tender.

For the sauce, smash and chop the chilli, and add the ginger and garlic and place it in a bowl. Pour in the hot chicken stock, light soya sauce, lemon juice, and sugar. Allow it to blend and cool.

For serving the Hainese chicken rice, arrange a bed of rice on a platter. Carve the chicken into slices and place on top of the rice. Drizzle sauce and garnish with coriander, spring onions, and red chilli.

*For chicken stock recipe see p xv.

Preparation time 15 mins
Cooking time 30 mins

Roasted Chicken with Tandoori Masala Serves 4

What do you do when you don't have a tandoor at home and you're craving some good ol roasted chicken? Either order out or serve yourself in half the time by cooking this recipe. The tandoori masala is a no brainer and once the chicken is marinated, use an oven or an open grill to serve this internationally famous Indian kebab.

1 kg **chicken (whole, skin on)**
¾ cup **hung curd**
1 tbsp **ginger paste**
1 tbsp **garlic paste**
Salt to taste

1 tbsp **lemon juice**
1 tbsp **Kashmiri chilli powder**
1 tsp **fenugreek leaves powder**
3 tbsp **mustard oil**

Pat dry the chicken. In a bowl, add mustard oil and then chilli powder. Mix well and add the hung yoghurt, ginger, garlic paste, lemon juice, salt, and fenugreek leaves powder.

Now carefully separate the skin from the meat and run this marinade under the skin of the chicken.

Apply generously to the breast and leg of the chicken. Leave aside for 20 minutes. Preheat the oven to 160°C and roast the chicken for 20 minutes. Now increase the heat to 190°C and cook for another 10 minutes or till the outer side is crispy.

Alternatively you can cook it on an open fire.

*Use a chilli powder that gives a deep red colour and is low on hotness.

Preparation time 55 mins
Cooking time 15 mins

Steamed Vegetable Bao (Buns) Serves 2

One of the most famous dim sums is the pork bun or pork bao. This vegetarian version is equally good and makes an excellent starter. But because it is light and healthy, make a few extra for a satisfying meal.

For the Dough
250 gm maida
40 gm sugar
15 gm white butter
10 gm baking powder
2 ½ tsp dry yeast
110 ml water
1 sheet butter paper

For the Stuffing
½ cup carrot, chopped
½ cup mushroom, chopped
½ cup baby corn, chopped
½ cup spring onions, chopped

2 tbsp oil
1 tbsp sesame oil
1 tbsp garlic, chopped
1 tsp fresh red chilli, chopped
1 tbsp soy sauce
2 tsp honey
¼ tsp star anise powder
¼ tsp clove powder
¼ tsp cinnamon powder
¼ tsp pepper powder
¼ tsp fennel powder
2 tsp cornstarch
Salt to taste

For the dough, mix yeast in warm water, add sugar and 1 tbsp of flour. Allow it to rest for 15 minutes. Now mix in the rest of the flour, baking powder, and butter.

Add water and make a soft dough and allow it to rise for 20 minutes. For the stuffing, make sure all the vegetables are very finely chopped. Heat oil and sesame oil and add garlic. Sauté lightly and immediately add all the chopped vegetables. Sauté a little and add soya sauce, honey, red chilli, and powdered spices.

Sauté and add cornstarch. Add salt if required. Sauté for 30 seconds and remove to a plate to cool completely. Make equal-sized balls of the dough (about the size of a golf ball). Place a spoonfull of stuffing in the centre and lightly shape back into a ball. Place the balls on a buttered paper and allow it to rise for about 20 minutes.

Prepare a steamer and steam the buns for 15 minutes. Remove and serve with soya sauce and chilli paste.

Preparation time 15 mins
Cooking time 10 mins

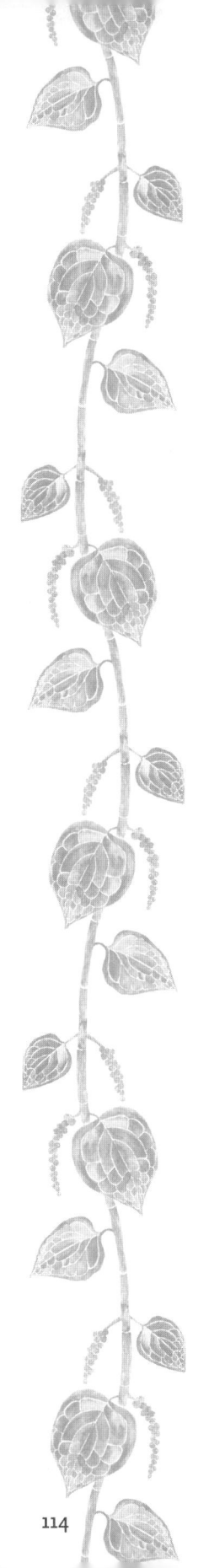

New Zealand's Beer Batter Fried Fish Serves 2

One of the best places on Earth is New Zealand and the best places to have fried fish there is on Plam Beach at Waiheke Island. In this recipe, New Zealand Beer blends beautifully with fish to give you one of the most delicious dishes ever.

4 fish fillets (100 gm each)
Salt to taste
Pepper to taste
2 tbsp lemon juice
2 cups flour (for the batter)

2 cups beer chilled
Oil for frying
4 lemon wedges
Flour for coating

Pat dry the fish fillet. Season with salt and pepper and squeeze some lemon juice over it.

Make a batter using flour, chilled beer, salt, and pepper. Make a thick batter and refrigerate it for 15 minutes. You can add a few ice cubes to the batter to make it really chilled.

Now dunk the fillets in flour and pat them lightly. Dip the fillet on both sides in the batter and deep fry in hot oil. Fry on medium heat till the outside puffs up and turns golden brown.

Serve hot with lemon wedges and potato wedges.

Preparation time **10 mins**

Basic Homemade Pasta Dough Makes 140 gm dough

This recipe shows you that Italian pasta is not so difficult to make after all. A simple ratio between flour and eggs can help you make the perfect pasta… every time.

100 gm **flour**
1 **large egg**

Make a well in the centre of the flour. Break both the eggs into it and mix with fingers. Make into a dough.

Now knead the dough for 5 minutes to develop elasticity in the dough. Wrap and keep aside to 15 minutes before using.

Preparation time 20 mins
Cooking time 10 mins

Ravioli Serves 2

Ravioli is pasta that is stuffed. You can stuff it with vegetables, meats, cheeses, and even eggs. You can prepare them and freeze for a few weeks.

280 gm **pasta dough***
¾ cup **hard cheese**, grated
1 ½ cup **pumpkin**, diced
3 tbsp **olive oil**
2 tbsp **onions**, chopped
2 tsp **fennel seeds**
A pinch of **pepper powder**

A pinch of **nutmeg**
Salt to taste

For the Sauce
3 tbsp **butter**
A sprig of **sage**
¼ cup **walnuts**

Heat oil in a pan and add onions and fennel. Sauté for 2 minutes and add the pumpkin. Season with salt, pepper, and nutmeg. Cook till pumpkin is tender and remove. Using the back of a spoon, mash up the pumpkin. Cool and mix in grated cheese.

Roll out the fresh pasta dough using a rolling pin. Flatten to about 1 mm thick. Using a round cutter, cut out round discs of about 2 ½' diameter.

Place a spoonfull of mashed pumpkin in the centre of a disc. Using your fingertips apply water on the edges of disc. Now carefully place another disc on top of the pasta and press gently. Press around the stuffing, lightly lifting it to give the shape of a head, working your way out towards the edges. Use a fork to press and seal the edges.

This will let out any air bubbles. Repeat for the rest of the dough. Boil water and add some oil to it. Drop the ravioli in boiling water and cook till it floats to the surface. Remove using a slotted spoon and place on a greased plate.

Heat pan and add butter. Add walnuts and sage and allow the butter to froth. Once it starts to turn brown, remove from heat and drizzle on top of the ravioli.

*For making pasta dough, see p 115.

Preparation time **10 mins**
Cooking time **12 mins**

Spaghetti Aglio Olio Serves 2

'Aglio' is Italian for garlic and 'olio' is oil. This simple dish from Abruzzo, Italy, has no sauce and yet has the most delightful taste. Try the dish with a nice white wine.

200 gm **spaghetti (dried)**
Salt to taste
6 tbsp **virgin olive oil**
1 tbsp **garlic, smashed and chopped**
1 tsp **chilli flakes**
1 tbsp **parsley, chopped**
3 tbsp **Parmesan cheese or any hard cheese***

In a deep pan, add water and let it boil. Add 2 tsp of salt and drizzle some oil. Drop the spaghetti in and allow it to boil till al dente. Usually, 7 to 8 minutes is the perfect boiling time.

Now strain the pasta and drizzle some oil over it again. Retain a cup of this water.

In a pan on a low flame, heat olive oil and chopped garlic. When it starts to lightly brown immediately add the pasta and a cup of water in which the pasta was boiled.

Add chilli flakes and sauté it till all moisture is absorbed. Season with salt, add parsley, and grated cheese. Toss and remove and immediately serve.

*Cheese is optional; any hard cheese can be used for this recipe if Parmesan is not available.

Preparation time **10 mins**
Cooking time **12 mins**

Tagliatelle with Mushrooms Serves 2

Tagliatelle, or flat ribbon pasta, is usually served in meat sauces. For this recipe, I have used mushrooms, garlic, and onions. Even though the dish is simple and explodes with flavours.

280 gm **pasta dough**
2 tbsp **olive oil**
1 ½ tbsp **butter**
1 tbsp **garlic, chopped**
1 tbsp **onion, chopped**
1 ½ cup **mushrooms, diced**

Pepper powder to taste
A sprig of thyme
1 cup **cream**
½ cup **cheese, grated**
¼ cup **parsley, chopped**
Salt to taste

Boil water and add salt and oil. Roll out the fresh pasta to 2 to 3 mm thickness. Cut 1 cm wide pasta strips and add it to the boiling water and cook for 5 minutes.

Drain water and drizzle some oil over the pasta.

Melt butter and add garlic and onions. Sauté till transparent. Now add thyme and mushroom and cook on a high flame. Add the cream, bring it to a boil, and add the pasta.

Season with salt and pepper, sprinkle grated cheese, and garnish with parsley.

Preparation time **20 mins**
Cooking time **35 mins**

Ratatouille Serves 2

This humble French dish of tomato, aubergine, peppers, and zucchini has captured the imagination of chefs around the world. Ratatouille is created in many ways, but here I give you the classic version of the same.

4 tbsp **olive oil**
1 ½ tbsp **garlic, chopped**
1 cup **onions, chopped**
10 **tomatoes, blanched**
½ cup **red capsicum, chopped**
½ cup **yellow capsicum, chopped**
2 sprigs **of basil**
6 **tomatoes, whole**

2 **yellow zucchinis**
2 **green zucchinis**
2 **Aubergines, long**
A sprig **of oregano**
3 tbsp **Parmesan cheese or any hard cheese**
Salt to taste
Pepper powder to taste

Take half of the blanched tomatoes and chop them. Make a purée from the rest of the tomatoes. Heat 3 tbsp of olive oil in a pan and add garlic and onions. Sauté for a while and now add red and yellow capsicum.

Cook for 2 minutes. Add basil leaves and then add chopped blanched tomatoes and tomato purée. Cook for 3 to 4 minutes. Season with salt and pepper. Remove from heat.

Separately using a sharp knife or a slicer, thinly slice aubergines, tomatoes, yellow and green zucchini, about 2 mm thick.

In a large baking dish, pour the sauce and sprinkle some grated cheese. Now place a slice of yellow zucchini, then tomato slice, then green zucchini and finally the aubergine slices. Repeat this till the entire surface of the dish is covered.

Sprinkle salt and pepper. Drizzle remaining olive oil and sprinkle oregano. Cover the dish with aluminum foil and bake in a preheated oven at 180°C for 25 minutes.

Remove the dish and serve immediately.

Preparation time **10 mins**
Cooking time **25 mins**

Baby Potatoes in Yoghurt Masala (Kashmiri Dum Aloo) Serves 2

God Bless Kashmir and its distinctive cuisine. This dish is almost always made wrong everywhere else in India, because it requires considerable skill and there's a lot of science involved. But I'll let you into a secret, which is that the twice-cooked potatoes soak up all the masala. This is the family recipe of Mr Rajiv Kaul, who is currently the president of the Leela Hotels in India. I had the opportunity to cook this recipe at a family wedding for the Kauls.

250 gm **baby potatoes**	½ tsp **turmeric powder**
Mustard oil for frying	1 ½ tbsp **coriander powder**
A pinch of **asafetida**	1 ½ tbsp **red chilli powder***
2 tsp **cumin seeds**	(Kashmiri mirch)
2 **black cardamom**	1 ½ cup **curd**
4 **cloves**	1 ½ tsp **dry ginger powder**
1 **cinnamon sticks**	**Salt** to taste
¼ cup **ginger** juliennes	**Coriander**, chopped for garnishing

Wash the potatoes and place them in a deep pan with cold water and some salt. Half boil them and remove. Allow them to cool and then peel them. Pierce with a toothpick or a fork at several places.

Heat mustard oil and deep fry them on medium heat for 3 minutes. Remove, wait for a minute and then fry again to make them crispy from the outside.

In a pan, pour about 3 tbsp of mustard oil and heat. Add asafoetida, black cardamom, cloves, cinnamon, and cumin. When the spices splutter, add turmeric, Kashmiri chilli powder, coriander powder, and ginger juliennes to the oil. Add ¼ cup water so that the spices do not burn. Sauté for a minute.

Add beaten curd to the above masala. Cook the yoghurt on a high flame and keep stirring for 1 to 2 minutes. This is done to make sure that the curd doesn't split. Now drop the potatoes and sprinkle salt and ginger powder. Cover with lid on a low flame for 10 minutes. The potatoes should absorb all the moisture. Garnish with green coriander leaves and serve hot.

*The chilli powder has to be a mild/sweet chilli powder like the deggi mirch.

Steamed Fish with Ginger and Light Soy (pg 100)

Chicken Schnitzel (pg 106)

New Zealand Beer Batter Fried Fish (pg 114)

Ravioli (pg 116)

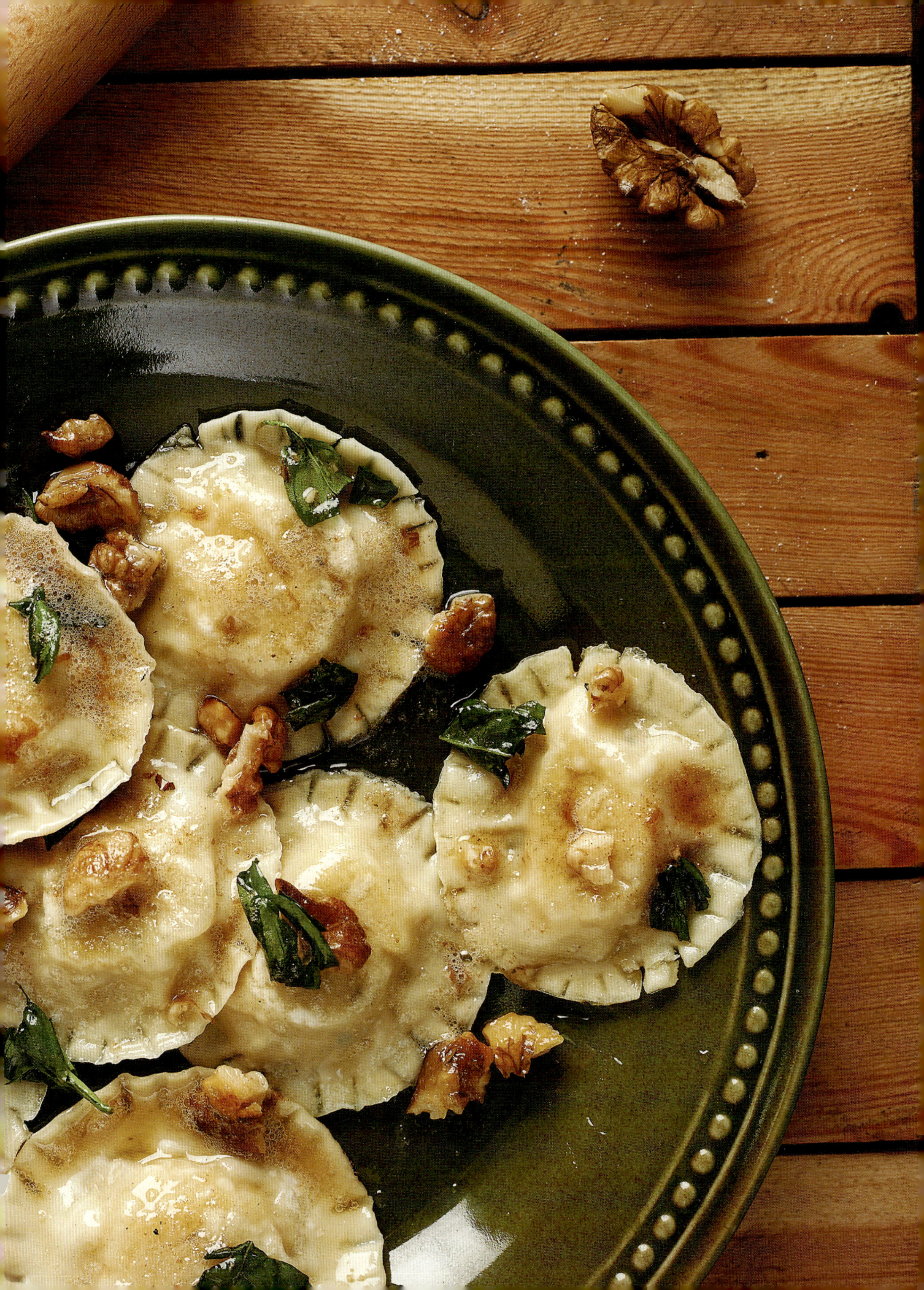

Husked Mung Beans with Peanuts (Moong Dal aur Moong Phalli) (pg 124)

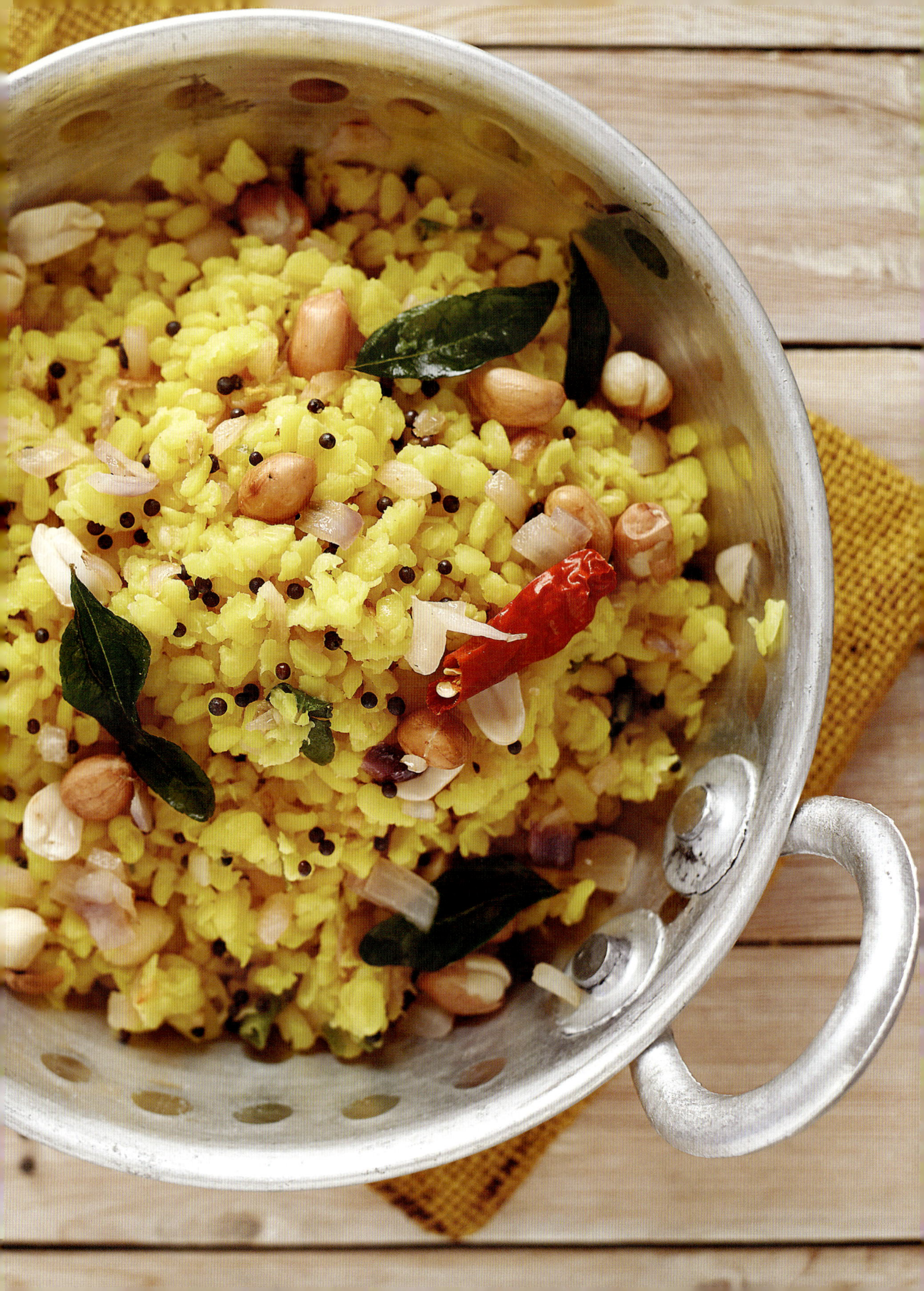

Bunny Chow (pg 125)

Preparation time **10 mins**
Cooking time **1 hr**

Dal Makhni Serves 10

What prompted me to include this recipe in the book is that a cook at home always wants to match the taste of his black lentil with what is served in the restaurants. This is the recipe of my multi-award winning Indian restaurant. You will love it.

250 gm **black urad dal**
200 gm **tomato purée***
125 gm **butter**
Red chilli powder (Kashmiri)**

2 tbsp **ginger paste**
2 tbsp **garlic paste**
100 ml **cream**
Salt to taste

Wash the dal and rub it with both hands to clean and remove as much of the black colour as you can. Soak overnight.

Change the water, add twice the amount of water and put it to boil. Boil the dal till it puffs open and becomes thick.

Now allow the dal to rest for 5 minutes. If the water is still very dark, drain a bit of that water.

Add ginger paste, garlic paste, Kashmiri chilli powder, butter, tomato puree, and salt. Start cooking and keep scrapping the bottom*** of the pan with a flat spoon.

Cook for 20 minutes and taste it. Check that there is no taste of any raw ingredients anymore in the dal. Finish with cream and immediately remove from fire.****

*Use a tomato purée can/tetra pack.

**Use a chilli powder that will give a nice bright cololur but is not too hot.

***Use a thick-bottomed pan or an iron griddle below a pan. This is done so that the dal does not stick to the bottom.

****You can add powdered dried fenugreek leaves (kasoori methi powder) to the dal before adding the cream and brown the chopped garlic in butter and add to the dal to finish it.

Preparation time 15 mins
Cooking time 15 mins

Menaskai Serves 2

How can pineapple be part of a spicy curry? I couldn't understand it when I first encountered this fascinating dish. This was one of my many awkward culinary moments in South India. But once I tasted it, I knew that there was no turning back. This dish will blow your pants away. Simply put, it's just SEXY.

1 ½ cups **pineapple, diced**
4 tbsp **coconut oil**
¼ tsp **asafoetida**
1 ½ tbsp **mustard seeds**
2 **dried red chillies**
2 sprigs **of curry leaves**
1 ½ cup **coconut, scraped**
2 tsp **sesame seeds**

1 tbsp **coriander seeds**
2 tsp **cumin**
1 tsp **red chilli powder**
½ tsp **turmeric**
2 tbsp **jaggery, grated**
Salt to taste
1 tbsp **tamarind pulp (optional)**

Heat 2 tbsp of coconut oil and add dried red chilli, ½ of the mustard seeds, sesame seeds, coriander seeds, and cumin. When they start to crackle, remove and mix them with the scrapped coconut. Use a little water to grind it to a fine paste.

Separately heat remaining coconut oil and add asafoetida, remaining mustard seeds, and curry leaves. Now add the diced pineapples and sauté for a minute. Add turmeric and red chilli powder, sauté and add the coconut paste. Add water and allow it to boil. Cook for 5 to 7 minutes.

Now add jaggery and a little tamarind to get the sweet and sour flavour. Serve hot.

If the pineapples are very sour you might not require tamarind. The same recipe can be made using raw mangoes.

Preparation time 10 mins
Cooking time 20 mins

Mustard Leaves with Roasted Almonds (Sarson aur Bhune Badam ki Subzi) Serves 4

Tossed spinach mixes with his best friends—garlic, butter and onions—to make a great dish.

3 cups mustard leaves (blanched)
2 tbsp butter
1 cup whole almonds (blanched and peeled)
2 tbsp onion, chopped
1 tbsp garlic, chopped
2 tsp green chillies, chopped
½ tsp turmeric
1 ½ tsp black pepper powder
2 tsp coriander powder
½ tsp soya leaves (dill leaves)
½ tsp salt

Lightly roast the almonds in the oven and keep them aside. Chop the soya leaves.

Heat butter and add the onion, garlic, green chilli and sauté them till the onions are transparent.

Add the blanched mustard leaves and sauté for 5 minutes. Add salt, turmeric, black pepper, and coriander powder and sauté for another minute.

Now toss in the dill and roasted almonds and remove immediately. Serve hot.

Preparation time **10 mins**
Cooking time **25 mins**

Husked Mung Beans with Peanuts (Moong Dal aur Moong Phalli) Serves 4

Moong dal when prepared dry has a rich, meaty flavour. This lentil goes well with paranthas and can also be used as a filling for a sandwich.

1 cup **husked mung beans (moong dal without skin)**
3 tbsp **ghee, clarified butter**
½ tsp **asafoetida**
2 tsp **mustard seeds**
1 **dried red chilli**
½ cup **curry leaves**
½ cup **peanuts, shelled and roasted**
1 **green chilli, chopped**
2 tsp **ginger, chopped**
½ cup **coconut, grated**
½ cup **onions, chopped**
1 tsp **turmeric**
1 ½ tsp **salt**
1 tbsp **lemon juice**
Green coriander, chopped for garnishing

Wash and soak the dal for 30 minutes. Now add double the amount of water and put it to boil. Add turmeric and ½ tsp of salt. Cook the dal till it is 3/4th done or al dente. Remove, strain, and keep aside.

Heat ghee in a pan and add the mustard seeds and dried red chilli. When they start to crackle, add asafoetida followed by curry leaves, ginger, and green chilli. Sauté on a low flame and add chopped onions.

Cook the onions till they are transparent. Now add turmeric and salt. Add dal and sauté till the dal is almost done.

To finish, add the grated coconut, roasted peanuts, and lemon juice. Check for seasoning. Serve hot garnished with chopped coriander.

Preparation time 15 mins
Cooking time 20 mins

Bunny Chow Serves 2

Bunny Chow was made famous by the Indian Baniya community in South Africa. There are several stories of how it came into existence. One such story claims that the Indians working in the restaurants of South Africa came up with this recipe because it was an effective way to pack a curry…in hollowed out bread. In South Africa, it is called Bunny or Kota.

5 tbsp oil
2 tsp cumin
2 tsp fennel seeds
2 sprigs of curry leaves
1 ½ cup onions, chopped
2 tbsp ginger, chopped
1 green chilli, chopped
¾ tsp turmeric
1 tsp red chilli powder

1 tbsp coriander powder
1 ½ cup tomatoes, chopped
1 cup potato cubes
2 cups French beans, diced
1 lemon wedge
2 tbsp coriander, chopped
1 bread loaf (unsliced)
Salt to taste

Heat oil in a thick-bottomed pan and add cumin and fennel seeds. When they start to crackle, add the curry leaves. Immediately add the chopped onions and ginger. Cook till the onions turn light brown.

Now add the chopped green chilli and ¼ cup of water. Immediately add turmeric, red chilli powder, and coriander powder. Cook till the oil surfaces again. Now add the tomatoes and cook for 3 minutes. Add diced potatoes and salt and sauté for 3 to 4 minutes. Add a little water so that it cooks without sticking to the bottom.

Add the beans and sauté. Cook till the oil surfaces. Now add sufficient water to make into a thick curry. Check for seasoning. Squeeze a lemon wedge and add chopped coriander leaves.

Take a loaf and cut it into 3" in height. Scoop out the centre*. Fill the cavity with the potato and beans curry. Replace the scooped out bread on top and serve immediately.

*When scooping out the centre, leave sufficient bread on the sides and bottom. My suggestion is to lightly toast the bread and then use it.

Preparation time 15 mins
Cooking time 15 mins

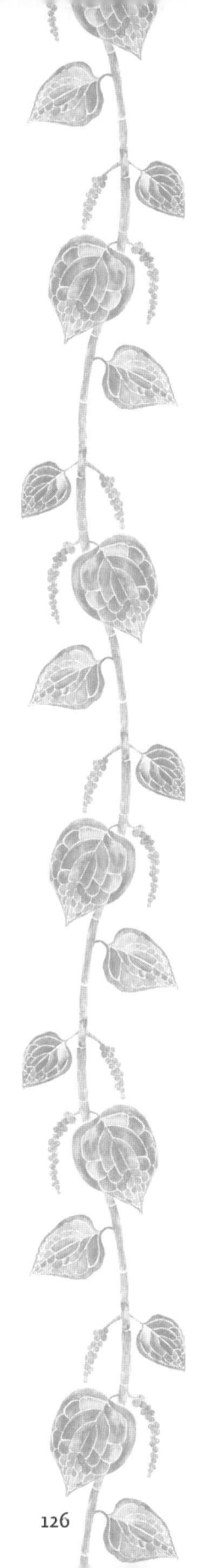

Stir Fried Vegetables in Light Garlic Sauce Serves 2

Light and simple, this Chinese dish brings the best out of vegetables. Remember to cook the veggies till they still have a crunch otherwise they will be soggy.

3 tbsp oil
1 ½ tbsp garlic, chopped
1 cup broccoli florets
2 cups spinach leaves
1 cup cauliflower florets
½ cup mushrooms, sliced
1 cup baby corn, diced
½ cup red capsicum, diced
½ cup yellow capsicum, diced
Pepper powder to taste
2 tsp sugar
1 tbsp soya sauce
1 tbsp vinegar
2 tbsp cornflour
1 tsp sesame oil
Salt to taste

Boil water and add some salt. Blanch spinach leaves and immediately dip them in cold water. Now partially boil the rest of the vegetables except the capsicums. Drain and keep aside.

Heat a wok/pan on low and add oil and garlic. Brown the garlic and immediately add the vegetables and capsicum. Stir the veggies for 2 minutes. Now add 2 cups water.

To this add salt, pepper, sugar, soya sauce, and vinegar. Add 4 tbsp of water in the cornflour and mix well.

Pour this cornflour into the vegetables and give it a quick boil. Once it thickens, remove from heat and drizzle sesame oil.

Preparation time 20 mins
Cooking time 30 mins

Khoye ki Subzi Serves 4

I came across this recipe by Vandana Sethi, a Chandigarh-based housewife, in a unique battle of taste conducted by Lufthansa on social media. I was part of the jury in this nation-wide hunt that drew over 1000 recipes from more than 100 towns across India. We selected this delicious entrée as the winner for its innovative use of traditional ingredients like khoya and phool makhane. This dish is now served onboard Lufthansa First and Business Class, celebrating India's culinary heritage. I think this is a great example of the fact that there is 'A Chef in Every Home'.

½ cup **potatoes**, cubed
½ cup **paneer cubes**, cottage cheese
½ cup **green peas**
½ cup **carrot**, cubed
½ cup **beans**, chopped
½ cup **popped lotus seeds** (phool makhana)
6 **almonds**
6 **cashewnuts**
1 cup **khoya***

For the Curry
¾ cup **oil**
2 tsp **cumin seeds**
2 **cloves**

1 small stick **cinnamon**
1 **black cardamom**
3 **green cardamoms**
5 **peppercorns**
2 tbsp **ginger garlic paste**
½ tsp **turmeric powder**
2 tsp **Kashmiri chilli powder**
1 tbsp **coriander powder**
1 cup **onions** (sliced and browned)
6 **tomatoes** (medium)
1 **green chilli**
2 to 3 cups **water**
1 tbsp **coriander**, chopped
Salt to taste

Sprinkle some salt on the potatoes and keep them aside. Deep fry the paneer, take it out, and place them in a bowl of water. Keep them in for 5 minutes and then take them out.

Fry almonds and cashewnuts in the same oil till light brown and keep aside.

Wash and wipe the potatoes and deep fry till they are golden brown. Deep fry the lotus seeds till they are crisp and keep aside.

In a pan, sauté khoya on a low flame for 2 to 3 minutes and keep aside. For the curry, grind brown onions with a little water and make a paste and keep aside.

Grind together tomatoes and green chilli to make a smooth paste.

Heat oil in a deep pan, add cumin seeds, clove, black and small cardamom, cinnamon, and black pepper. Sauté for few seconds and add ginger garlic paste. Cook for 2 minutes.

Add turmeric, coriander powder, red chilli powder, and salt to ¼ cup of water. Add this to the ginger garlic paste.

Cook on a low heat till the oil separates. Now add the brown onion paste and sauté for 2 minutes. Add tomato puree and cook till the oil separates.

Now add sautéed khoya and cook for 5 minutes. Add peas, carrots, and beans and cook for 4 to 5 minutes.

Add the potatoes, paneer, popped lotus seeds, almonds, and cashewnuts. Mix well. Add 2 to 3 cups of water and bring to a boil. Cook on a low flame till the carrots are tender.

Garnish with coriander leaves. Serve hot with Indian breads or rice.

*Khoya is reduced milk solids.

Sweet Tooth: Desserts

Preparation time 15 mins
Cooking time 15 mins

Bedtime Chocolate Shots Serves 2

Chocolates always help in lifting up your spirits. Here are three different flavours of chocolate shots—dark chocolate with chilli, fennel with white chocolate, and citrus with milk chocolate. This recipe is a great start to a romantic conversation and is a perfect end after a good meal.

For Chilli Dark Shot
100 gm dark chocolate
10 gm cocoa powder
100 ml cream
100 ml milk
1 fresh red chilli

For Fennel Cardamom White Shot
120 gm white chocolate
100 ml cream
100 ml milk
1 tsp fennel seeds
¼ tsp cardamom powder

For Orange Cinnamon Milk Shot
110 gm milk chocolate
100 ml cream
100 ml milk
1 tbsp orange rind, grated
¼ tsp cinnamon powder

For chilli dark shot, mix cream, milk, cocoa powder, slit chilli, and dark chocolate in a pan and put on a low heat. Once the chocolate melts, strain the chocolate and pour in shot glasses. Serve while it is still warm.

For fennel cardamom white shot, mix cream, milk, white chocolate, fennel seeds, and cardamom powder in a pan and put on a low heat. Once the chocolate melts, turn off the heat and keep aside to allow the flavours to infuse for 2 minutes. Strain and pour in shot glasses and serve while it is still warm.

For orange cinnamon milk shot, mix cream, milk, milk chocolate, orange rind, and cinnamon powder in a pan and put on low heat. Once the chocolate melts, turn off the heat and keep aside to allow the flavours to infuse. Strain and pour in shot glasses and serve while it is still warm.

Preparation time 15 mins
Cooking time 45 mins

Pavlova Serves 2

Pavlova is a meringue-based dessert named after the legendary ballet dancer Anna Pavlova. A delectable dessert that is crisp from the outside and soft on the inside. It is best served with freshly whipped cream and berries.

100 gm **egg white**	**For the Topping**
100 gm **sugar (fine grain)**	200 ml **cream (unsweetened**
100 gm **icing sugar**	**for whipping)**
2 tsp **vinegar/lemon juice**	1 tsp **vanilla extract**
2 tsp **cornflour**	**Icing sugar for dusting**
1 **butter paper**	12 **berries***

Heat the oven to 120°C. In a clean bowl, add the egg whites and whisk it. It is preferable to use an electric blender. Start whisking at a slow speed and build it up gradually till the egg whites fluff up to soft peaks.

Now slowly add grain sugar and icing sugar one spoon at a time and keep whisking it. Repeat till all the sugar is used up and completely dissolved. Whisk till the whites are stiff; if you upturn the bowl the egg whites should not fall. Quickly whisk in cornflour and vinegar.

In a baking tray, add butter paper and using a large spoon pour out the stiff glossy whites. Very gently flatten (1" thick) out in a round shape. Remember, it does not have to be perfectly round. Bake in the pre-heated oven for 45 minutes, then turn off the oven and let it rest for half an hour inside. Remove and allow it to cool completely. Remove the butter paper as well.

Separately whisk cream and vanilla extract till it is stiff. Smear the cream on top of the Pavlova. Garnish with quartered strawberries and drizzle icing sugar on top of them. Serve immediately.

*You can use any fruit of your choice; any sharp tasting fruit will go very well with this dessert.

The ratio of egg whites to sugar is 1:2, which means that if you use 50 gm of egg whites then you need to add 100 gm of sugar for making the Pavlova.

Preparation time 10 mins
Cooking time 20 mins

Vanilla Sauce Makes 2 cups

Also known as crème anglaise' or custard sauce, vanilla sauce has a very soothing flavour. The creamy texture of the sauce is best enjoyed by pouring over warm pound cakes or serving with ice creams and fruit salads.

1 cup **milk**
1 cup **cream**
1 tsp **vanilla extract**

7 to 8 **egg yolks**
½ cup **sugar**

Mix milk, cream, and vanilla extract together in a pan and give it a boil. Simmer for 2 to 3 minutes. Remove from heat.

Separately mix egg yolks and sugar in a bowl and whisk till all the sugar is dissolved. Now gently pour the milk over the eggs and keep whisking.

Pour the contents back in the pan and simmer for 2 to 3 minutes. Keep stirring all the time. Remove from heat and strain the sauce into a clean bowl.

Immediately place this bowl in iced water to cool it. The sauce should be of a pouring consistency yet should coat the back of the spoon.

Preparation time **10 mins**
Cooking time **20 mins**

Potli Masala Crème Brûlée Serves 2

This is crème brulee flavoured with a mixed bag of spices (also called potli). Make a personalized bag of spices with all your favourite flavours. This French dessert gets a desi twist with the subtle flavours of spices.

1 cup **milk (full cream)**
1 cup **cream**
1 tsp **vanilla extract**
7 to 8 **egg yolks**
½ cup **sugar**
1 to 2 tsp **screw pine flower essence (kewra)**

2 tbsp **sugar (fine grain)**

Potli Masala
½ tsp **cinnamon powder**
½ tsp **fennel powder**
½ tsp **cardamom powder**

Mix milk, cream, and vanilla extract together in a pan and give it a boil, then let in simmer for 2 to 3 minutes. Remove from heat.

Separately mix yolks and sugar in a bowl and whisk till all the sugar is dissolved. Now gently pour the milk over the whisked eggs and keep whisking. Pour the contents back in the pan and let it simmer for 2 to 3 minutes. Keep stirring all the time.

Remove from heat and add the potli masala and kewra water. Strain the contents and pour in oven-proof bowls. Place these bowls in a deep roasting tray filled with hot water up till 3/4th of the cups.

Bake in a preheated oven at 160°C for 35 minutes or till it becomes firm. Remove from oven and allow it to cool. Now keep it in the refrigerator to completely chill it.

Sprinkle fine grain sugar over the crème brulee and using a blowtorch caramelize the sugar for a crunchy top. Alternatively, in a pan heat sugar on low heat and caramelize it. Immediately pour this over the crème brûlée.

Preparation time **10 mins**
Cooking time **20 mins**

Ginger Chocolate Florentines Makes 10

Florentines are biscuits made from nuts, flour, and sugar. They are thin slices of heaven that can be dipped in chocolate sauce.

100 gm **butter (unsalted)**
100 gm **sugar**
2 tsp **ginger powder**
110 gm **flour**
120 gm **pistachio, broken**
120 gm **almonds, broken**
120 gm **cashewnuts, broken**
200 gm **chocolate**

For Baking
1 sheet aluminum foil
Oil for greasing the baking tray
1 butter paper

Wisk butter and sugar together until the butter is soft and fluffy. Now mix in the flour, ginger powder, and the nuts.

On a baking tray, spread a sheet of aluminum foil and lightly oil it. Make equal-sized, small balls of the dough and place on the aluminum sheet. Bake this in a preheated oven at 180°C for about 7 minutes. When the Florentines start getting some colour, remove them from the oven and allow them to cool.

Melt chocolate and dip half of the Florentine in this molten chocolate and place on a butter paper. Allow them to cool, remove, and serve.

Preparation time **10 mins**
Cooking time **20 mins**

Nan Khatai with Cinnamon and Orange Rind Makes 20

In India, Nan Khatai is an eggless cookie made with flour, sugar, and butter. It is a very delicate and addictive cookie and this recipe gives it a fresh twist.

250 gm **unsalted butter**
250 gm **icing sugar**
250 gm **flour**
½ tsp **baking powder**
3 tbsp **orange rind**
½ tsp **cinnamon powder**

Soften the butter and mix with the sugar. Mix vigorously and then gently fold in the flour, baking powder, orange rind, and cinnamon powder. Work it into a dough.

Now grease a baking tray and sprinkle some flour. Make equal-sized, round balls of the dough and place them on the tray.

Bake the nan khatai at a temperature of 140°C for 20 to 25 minutes. Take them out of the oven and allow them to cool.

You can store them in an airtight jar.

Preparation time 10 mins
Cooking time 10 mins

Chocolate Sauce or Ganache Makes 2 cups

Ganache is made from chocolate and cream and has multiple uses. It can be used as an icing, a filling, or a sauce, glaze, or even for making pralines. It can be made with dark, milk, or white chocolate.

125 gm **cream**
125 gm **dark chocolate**

Break the chocolate in a bowl and keep in a warm place so that it softens. Pour the cream in a pan, bring to a boil, and pour it over the chocolate.

Allow it to rest for 2 to 3 minutes and then whisk it evenly.

Use this sauce as a topping for cakes, as a sauce for pouring, or to make chocolate truffles.

Bedtime Chocolate Shots (pg 130)

Pavlova (pg 131)

Nan Khatai with Cinnamon and Orange Rind (pg 135)

Potli Masala Crème Brûlée (pg 133)

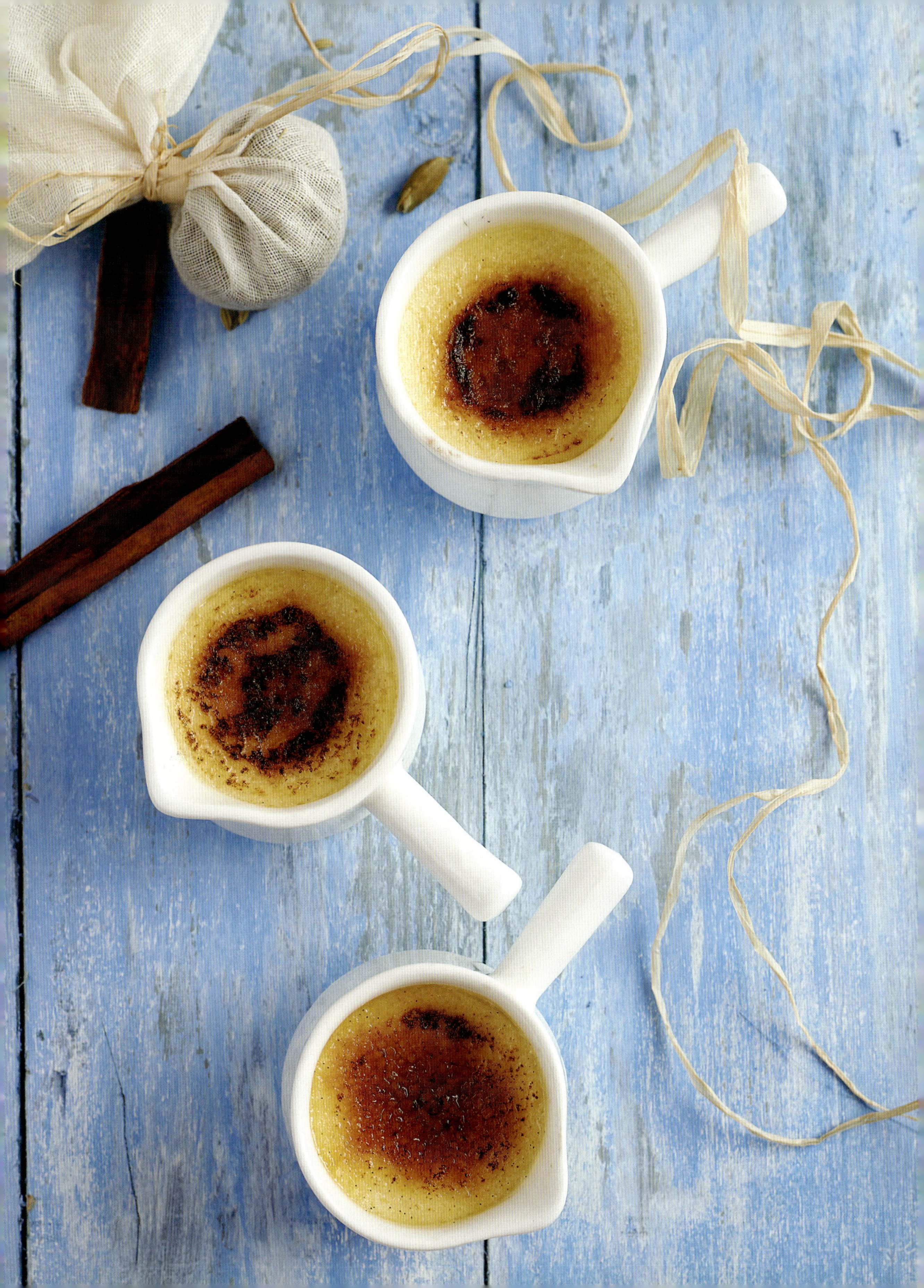

Paan Supari Pannacotta (pg 141)

Fruit and Nut Chocolate Cake (pg 145)

Ande ki Lauz with Lemon Curd (pg 146)

Preparation time 10 mins
Cooking time 20 mins

Dark Chocolate Truffles Makes 20

Chocolate truffles are small chocolate tit-bits that have a chocolate ganache. These truffles are sometimes flavoured and stuffed as well.

250 gm **dark chocolate**
125 gm **cream**
½ cup **cocoa powder**

For Fillings and Flavour Variation
50 gm **aam papad sweet**
    (dried mango sheets)
75 ml **rum**

Chop up the chocolate in a bowl and put it in a pan. Give the cream a quick boil and then add it to the chocolate. Stir well till all the chocolate dissolves. Strain and refrigerate for about an hour.

Chop up aam papad. Remove the chocolate from the fridge and using a spoon, scoop out some on your palm. Stuff some aam papad in the thick chocolate and roll it up. Refrigerate again for 15 minutes.

Now remove and dust with cocoa powder.

For making rum flavoured truffles, mix the cream, chocolate, and add the rum and mix evenly. Now refrigerate and shape into round balls.

Preparation time **10 mins**
Cooking time **20 mins**

White Chocolate Truffles Makes 20

White chocolate truffles flavoured with fennel seeds are my personal favourite. These tit-bits of chocolate are perfect for serving at festivities and can be easily made at home.

250 gm + 100 gm **white chocolate**
125 gm **cream**

For Flavours
1 tbsp **fennel seeds**

Chop up 250 gm of chocolate. Crush the fennel and add to the cream.

Give the cream a quick boil and then add it to the chocolate. Stir well till all the chocolate dissolves. Strain and refrigerate for about an hour.

Remove the chocolate from the fridge and using a spoon scoop out some on your palm. Roll it up and refrigerate again for 15 minutes.

Melt the remaining 100 gm of chocolate in a microwave or in a double boiler. Dip the refrigerated truffle in molten white chocolate and immediately take it out and put on a wire rack or butter paper.

Refrigerate and allow the chocolate to set.

Preparation time **10 mins**
Cooking time **20 mins**

Caramel sauce Makes 1 cup

Caramelized sugar and fresh cream blends together to give you an unforgettable toffee flavour.

1 cup **sugar**
¼ cup **water**
1 tsp **lemon juice**

1 ¼ cup **cream**
50 gm **unsalted butter**

Put sugar, water, and lemon juice in a pan and cook till the sugar gets a nice golden, caramel colour.

Remove the pan from fire and add the cream. Mix it well till it turns into a sauce consistency. Now drop in the butter and mix it nicely.

Transfer to a bowl.

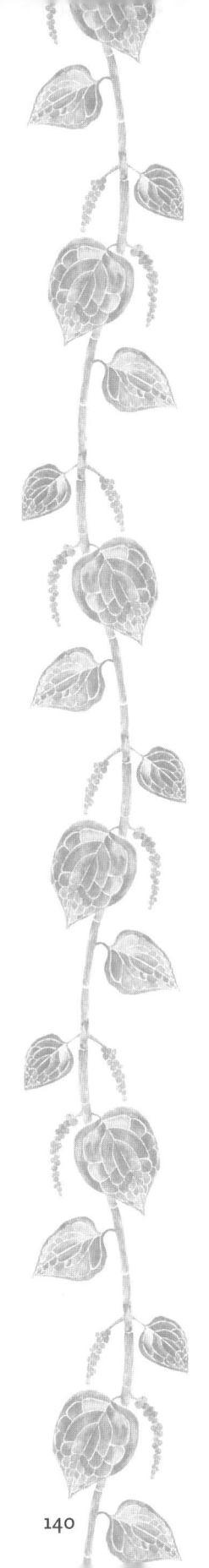

Preparation time **10 mins**
Cooking time **20 mins**

Pastry Creme Makes 2 cups

Pastry cream or custard is used as a filling for various desserts. The creamy and velvety thick coating will definitely make you go for another spoonfull.

350 ml **milk**
250 ml **cream**
1 tsp **vanilla extract**
7 to 8 **egg yolks**

125 gm **sugar**
100 gm **cornflour**
70 gm **unsalted butter**

Mix 250 ml milk, cream, and vanilla extract together in a pan and give it a boil. Let it simmer for 2 to 3 minutes and remove from heat.

In another bowl, mix eggs yolks and sugar and whisk till all the sugar dissolves.

Now gently pour the milk over the whisked eggs and keep whisking. Pour the contents back in the pan and let it simmer for 2 to 3 minutes. Keep stirring all the time.

Mix the remaining 100 ml milk with cornflour and pour it very slowly into the custard. Keep stirring vigorously so that it thickens; it needs to be very thick.

Immediately remove from heat and transfer the contents into a bowl. Place this bowl in chilled water. Keep stirring and add the butter. Mix well till the butter dissolves. Allow it to cool completely before using.

Preparation time 15 mins
Cooking time 10 mins

Paan Supari Pannacotta Serves 10

Betel leaf and the Indian betel nut is a mouth freshener with a unique zing. In India, it is customary for the hosts to offer their guests this after dinners. This dessert takes on the Italian pannacotta and gives it a fresh avatar.

500 ml **fresh cream**
75 ml **sugar (fine grain)**
15 gm **gelatin**
10 **betel leaf**

1 tbsp **betel nut mixture, supari mixture**
2 tsp **kewra water***
25 gm **gulkand****

Soak gelatin with equal amount of cold water in a bowl and keep aside.

Pour the cream in a pan and bring it to a boil. Remove from heat and add sugar and kewra water. Let it rest till it is turns warm.

In the meantime, put the betel leaf in a blender and add 2 ice cubes. Make a puree but make sure it does not turn brown.

Heat the gelatin in a pan over a fire or in a microwave till it turns liquid. Add it to the warm cream. Add the betel leaf puree and supari.

Pour the mixture in a mould of your choice and refrigerate for 2 hours. Then, demould and serve topped with some gulkand.

* Remember, intensity of kewra water differs from one brand to another, so use according to its strength.

** Gulkand is rose petals wilted in sugar. You can find it in a grocery store or paan shop.

Preparation time 5 mins
Cooking time 15 mins

Berry Compote Makes 2 cups

Compote is a French word meaning mixture. Compote was originally made with fruits cooked in sugar with certain spices and had in the evening with tea. Today, compote sauce is served as a dessert accompaniment. Berries are my personal favourite and this compote can be used with pancakes for breakfast or poured over ice creams or simply as a side sauce with desserts.

150 gm **frozen blueberry**
100 gm **frozen raspberry**
100 gm **frozen blackberry**

300 gm **sugar**
10 ml **lemon juice**

Add all the berries and sugar in a clean and dry pan. Cook for 15 to 20 minutes on a low flame.

Add lemon juice and bring it to a boil. Let it cool and store for future use.

Preparation time **15 mins**
Cooking time **10 mins**

Chocolate Mousse (with Egg) Serves 10

Eggs are a very important component in baking. Chocolate mousse with eggs makes for a thicker, heavier and denser flavour and feel than mousse without the eggs.

500 gm **dark chocolate**
5 **egg yolks**
50 gm **caster sugar**
150 ml **milk**
300 gm **whipped cream**
8 gm **gelatin**

Whip cream to a soft peak consistency. Soak gelatin in 20 ml water and keep aside.

In a clean bowl, place egg yolks, sugar, and milk. Put this on a double boiler. Whisk till the egg becomes thick and still has pouring consistency.

Melt chocolate separately and add the molten chocolate into the eggs. Then add 8 gm of gelatin. Wait till the mixture comes down to room temperature. Now fold in whipped cream and pipe mousse into a mould or glass of your choice.

Warm the mango pulp and add 10 gm of bloomed gelatin and set it on top of the chocolate mousse. Refrigerate for 4 hours and serve cold.

Preparation time 15 mins
Cooking time 30 mins

Bread n Butter Pudding Serves 4

This hearty pudding has its roots in England. It is easy to make and the warm feel of the bread and creamy custard is exciting. You can add candied peel and raisins soaked in rum or whiskey.

10 eggs
150 gm caster sugar
2 tsp vanilla extract
1 litre milk

100 gm butter
200 gm white bread
50 gm raisins
50 gm cashewnuts

Boil the milk with sugar and vanilla extract and remove from heat. Allow it to cool till it is just warm. Now add the beaten eggs and strain the mixture.

Cut the sides of the bread. Arrange the bread in a baking mould and pour melted butter on top.

Add cashew, raisin, and the above milk. Place the mould in a deep tray and fill it with water till it is 3/4th of the mould height. Now bake in a preheated oven at 150°C for 25 to 30 minutes.

To check if it is done, slide a knife into the centre of the pudding—if it comes out clean the pudding is baked. Remove and serve warm.

Preparation time 20 mins
Cooking time 40 mins

Fruit and Nut Chocolate Cake Makes a 1 kg cake

Dried fruits and chocolate complement each other in any form. This is an easy recipe of the all time favourite chocolate cake. No stress, just prepare in good quantities and keep it for a couple of weeks.

150 gm **flour**
150 gm **sugar**
200 gm **butter (unsalted)**
3 **eggs**
15 gm **cocoa powder**
40 gm **dark chocolate**

20 ml **milk**
2 gm **baking powder**
30 gm **raisins**
30 gm **pista, chopped**
30 gm **cashewnuts, chopped**
100 ml **rum (optional)**

Melt chocolate in a double boiler and keep aside. Soak raisins in rum.

Smear a little butter in a baking pan and dust with flour and keep aside. Preheat the oven to 170°C.

Add butter and sugar in a clean bowl. Whisk the butter and sugar together till the sugar almost dissolves. Keep whisking and add one egg after the other till all the eggs are in.

Add molten chocolate. Now fold in the flour gently in a criss-cross lifting motion. Add milk, nuts, and rum-soaked raisins. Pour the batter into the prepared mould and bake at 170°C for 40 minutes.

Preparation time 20 mins
Cooking time 20 mins

Ande ki Lauz with Lemon Curd Serves 4

This is a classic Hyderabadi dish made with eggs and I have paired it with French lemon curd, which is sour and creamy. The lauz comes out much like a cake and the almonds give it a deep and rich flavour.

For Ande ki Lauz
75 gm almonds
A few strands of saffron
150 gm sugar
75 gm khoya (reduced milk solids)
8 eggs
50 gm desi ghee
Refined flour for dusting

For Lemon Curd
25 ml lemon juice
50 gm butter
50 gm sugar
2 to 3 egg yolks (50 gm approx)

Prepare a deep baking tray by brushing with ghee and dusting with flour.

Soak the almonds overnight to loosen its skin. Alternatively give the almonds a quick boil, strain, and remove the skin. Make a paste out of it using as little water as possible.

Pour a tablespoon of hot water in saffron and allow the saffron to release its colour.

In the meantime, rub together khoya and sugar until it is creamy. Separately whisk eggs until they are light and frothy. Add khoya, almond paste, saffron, and molten desi ghee to the whisked eggs and mix well.

Pour the batter in the prepared tray and bake in an oven at 180°C for 10 to 12 minutes. To check if it is done, slide a knife into it and if it comes out clean it is cooked or else bake for another 2 to 3 minutes.

For the lemon curd, mix together egg yolks, sugar, and lemon juice in a bowl. Place the bowl in a pan of simmering water (double boiler) and keep whisking for about 8 to 10 minutes so that it becomes thick.

Now remove from heat and gradually add softened butter little by little, till all the butter is in. Allow this to cool and then refrigerate.

Once the lauz is baked, allow it to cool. Remove from the tray. Smear the lemon curd on the lauz and serve it as a dessert or as a great high tea accompaniment.

The lauz rises quickly and after you remove it from the oven it will sink in a little.

Preparation time **10 mins**
Cooking time **10 mins**

Caramel Bananas Serves 4

Caramel and bananas with a hint of salt is a match made in heaven. Try and resist it.

4 **bananas**
1 cup **sugar**
1 tsp **lemon juice**

¾ cup **cream**
50 gm **butter**
½ tsp **cinnamon powder**

Slit the bananas lengthwise.

In a pan, melt butter, sugar, and lemon juice. Add the bananas and cook on low heat till the sugar dissolves and caramelizes. Add the cream immediately.

Swirl the pan and allow the cream and sugar to mix. Sprinkle cinnamon powder and remove to a serving dish.

Preparation time 5 mins

5-minute Yoghurt Ice Cream Serves 4

This is the quickest ice cream recipe ever. So quick that even your kids can make it. Guaranteed to bring out the child in you.

400 gm **yoghurt (hung and chilled)**	1 ½ tbsp **honey**
400 gm **berries (frozen)**	4 tbsp **almonds (toasted and broken)**

Put together the yoghurt, honey, and berries in a food processor. Blend all the ingredients together and immediately scoop it out and serve with toasted almonds. Or transfer to a container and deep freeze.

Make sure the berries are frozen and the yoghurt chilled. You might want to put the yoghurt in the deep freezer for half hour before using it.

The food processor might be sluggish initially but keep scrapping the sides until everything becomes one semi-frozen mass.

List of Recipes

SMACKY STARTERS

Asparagus and Cherry Tomato Cheese Tarts pg 40
Baked Potato Skins pg 27
Chicken Porcupine pg 29
Crispy Shredded Lamb (Gosht ki Sev) pg 37
Falafel pg 19
Flat Bread with Pesto and Cottage Cheese (Paneer) pg 35
Fried Fish Amritsari pg 42
Fried Mozzarella Sticks with Tomato Sauce pg 25
Golden Fried Prawns pg 38
Harissa Marinated Grilled Prawns pg 33
Hummus: 3 Ways pg 21
Keerai Vadai pg 41
Lotus Stem Crisps (Kurkuri Kamal Kakdi) pg 36
Melon n' Cheese pg 24
Mini Cheese Calzones pg 26
Moutabal pg 22
Mushroom and Walnuts on Crisp Bread pg 31
Mutton Varuval pg 30
Pea and Potato Croquette pg 20
Quesadilla pg 34
Queso Fundido pg 32
Raw Papaya Kebabs with Mango Salsa pg 18
Shammi Kebabs pg 39
Shish Taouk pg 23
Spinach and Cheese Stuffed Mushrooms pg 28

THE ESSENTIALS: CONDIMENTS, DIPS, RELISHES, CHUTNEYS

Aubergine and Peanut Chutney pg 48
Charmoula Sauce pg 47

Churan Chutney pg 52
Coconut Chutney pg 47
Guacamole pg 53
Lemon Water Pickle pg 52
Mayonnaise pg 53
Mint and Spring Onion Chutney pg 51
Olive Tapenade pg 49
Pesto pg 54
Pineapple Chutney pg 44
Red Chilli Paste pg 44
Sour Cream pg 46
Tahini pg 45
Tahini Sauce pg 45
Toum (Lebanese Garlic Sauce) pg 50
Tzatziki pg 46

HEALTHY AND FUN MENUS FOR KIDS

ABC Smoothie pg 58
Baked Mac n' Cheese pg 63
Baked Chicken and Tomato with Potato Mash pg 66
Baked Yoghurt pg 68
Chocolate Mousse with Citrus Rind pg 64
Chicken Tenders pg 71
Cream of Broccoli Soup pg 65
Creamy Avocado and Cucumber Soup pg 61
Easy Cupcakes pg 73
Finger Sandwiches: Two Ways pg 70
French Toast pg 59
Granola Parfait: Two Ways pg 60
Rosemary Potato Wedges pg 72
Scrambled Eggs with Cheese, Spring Onions, Broccoli, and Tomatoes on Toast pg 57
Tomatoes and Pickled Beet Salad pg 62
Tomato Bruschetta pg 69

SALADS AND SOUPS FOR THE SOUL

Apple Walnut and Greens pg 79
Aubergine, Pomegranate and Garlic Yoghurt Salad pg 80

Bhutte ka Shorba with Chilli Butter Popcorns (Indian Corn Soup) pg 82
Chicken Eggdrop Soup pg 81
Kaddu ka Shorba (Pumpkin Soup) pg 83
Kimchi: Done My Way pg 78
Minestroni pg 84
Raw Papaya and Raw Mango Salad pg 76
Rocket Salad with Stewed Figs and Cheese pg 77

BREADS AND RICE

Chicken Machboos pg 94
Khoba Roti pg 88
Khoye ka Parantha pg 87
Olive Parantha pg 89
Pita Bread pg 91
Roti Jala pg 90
Stir Fried Rice pg 92
Tortilla (Mexican flat bread) pg 86
Tawa Pulao pg 95
Yakhni Pulao pg 93

HEARTY MAIN COURSES

Baby Potatoes in Yoghurt Masala (Kashmiri Dum Aloo) pg 120
Basic Homemade Pasta Dough pg 115
Bunny Chow pg 125
Charmoula Rubbed Grilled Fish pg 98
Char Siu Mutton Chops pg 101
Chicken and Potato Stew pg 109
Chicken Cacciatora pg 108
Chicken Schnitzel pg 106
Dal Makhni pg 121
Filipino Chicken Adobo pg 107
Goulash pg 103
Hainese Chicken Rice pg 110
Husked Mung Beans with Peanuts (Moong Dal aur Moong Phalli) pg 124
Khoye ki Subzi pg 127
Lamb Skewers with Yoghurt Dip pg 104
Menaskai pg 122
Mustard Leaves with Roasted Almonds pg 123

(Sarson aur Bhune Badam ki Subzi)
New Zealand's Beer Batter Fried Fish pg 114
Prawns Moilee pg 99
Ratatouille pg 119
Ravioli pg 116
Roasted Chicken with Tandoori Masala pg 112
Sheppard's Pie pg 102
Soy Marinated Chicken with Chilli Coriander pg 105
Spaghetti Aglio Olio pg 117
Steamed Fish with Ginger and Light Soy pg 100
Steamed Vegetable Bao (Buns) pg 113
Stir Fried Vegetables in Light Garlic Sauce pg 126
Tagliatelle with Mushrooms pg 118

SWEET TOOTH: DESSERTS

Ande ki Lauz with Lemon Curd pg 146
Bedtime Chocolate Shots pg 130
Berry Compote pg 142
Bread n Butter Pudding pg 144
Caramel Bananas pg 148
Caramel Sauce pg 139
Chocolate Mousse (with Egg) pg 143
Chocolate Sauce or Ganache pg 136
Dark Chocolate Truffles pg 137
Fruit and Nut Chocolate Cake pg 145
Ginger Chocolate Florentines pg 134
Nan Khatai with Cinnamon and Orange Rind pg 135
Paan Supari Pannacotta pg 141
Pastry Crème pg 140
Pavlova pg 131
Potli Masala Crème Brûlée pg 133
Vanilla Sauce pg 132
White Chocolate Truffles pg 138
5-minute Yoghurt Ice Cream pg 149

Acknowledgements

A man's success is because of the collective efforts of all the people who care for him. I owe all my knowledge and interest for cooking to my big family where all the men love to cook. My fondest and cherished memories are of my dad, granddad, and uncles cooking together in our humble kitchen at home.

I thank my grandfather, Late Shri Harbans Lal Kapur, for instilling in me the basics of cooking. I will always remember how he taught me to crumb an aloo tikki and miss his way of making kulfi with leftover barfis. The most famous chef in our home is my chacha, Mr Vipin Kapur—his supreme sense of taste is unparralled. His food is always the talking point in the family. I still remember how he would patiently cook meat and pulaos. I did learn a trick or two from his style.

My dad, Mr Deepak Kapur, is the innovative type and I agree there have been few successes and a couple of failures in his life. But the fact that he never gave up innovating is the reason he keeps cooking again and again. He is a very methodical man and it was he who showed me how to cook stuffed omelets. He always said that a good omelet must never be brown. And how right he is!

Thank you to my fufaji, Mr Kamal Madhok. He would make mango ice cream every time we went to his house for the summer holidays. I could never figure out how and why his fresh mango ice cream tasted so good. Our family friend, Mr Swaranjeet Singh, is a big foodie. Both our families would get together and go out for picnics to the India Gate lawns in the Delhi winters. He would carry his charcoal grill to the lawns and I would assist him with barbequing rather than playing with the other kids. It was a good start for me.

All the lecturers in my college, especially my food production head, Mr TK Razdan, and pastry head, Mr Rohit Arora, took special interest in nurturing me. In my second year, Mr Sanjeev Verma taught me lessons on cooking food in large quantities and Mr Vinod Sidhu hand-held me and taught me baking and pastry.

Chef Arvind Saraswat, the Corporate Chef of Taj Hotels (2000), and Chef Nita Nagraj, Executive Chef Taj Palace, Delhi (2000), are the two chefs who took me under their wing. I owe so much to them for their intense training programmes. They are one of the best chefs in our country and I am blessed to have trained under them.

My sincerest thanks to Mr Raj Singh Gehlot and his family for giving me a beautiful hotel to start with. The Honourable Chairman Emeritus CP Krishnan Nair, the founder Chairman of the Leela Group of Hotels and Resorts; he is an institution in himself and has created Dharmas of hoteliering, which are part of my lifestyle. Mr Rajiv Kaul, President of the Leela Group, is the driving force behind my success as a chef and as a television host. My mentor Michel Koopman, General Manager of the Leela Ambience Gurgaon Hotel and Residencies, for making this one of the most successful hotels in India.

A Note on the Author

Kunal is one of the most celebrated faces of Indian cuisine today. He is chef extraordinaire, TV show host, winner of several culinary awards, and now an author!

Kunal is the proud recipient of the prestigious Sir Edmund Hillary Fellowship 2012 from the Government of New Zealand in the field of Food & Beverage. This fellowship/award is awarded every year to an individual for his contribution in his respective field.

He is also in the Elite Category of Star Chefs, representing Indian cuisine on board Lufthansa Airlines with his specialty menus for first and business class.

Jigs Kalra, the scion of Indian food, said, 'Kunal is the next big guy in Kebabs & Curries in India.' He has won Best Restaurant awards seven times in his career of thirteen years. Kunal is recognized among the Best Chefs in India by *India Today*. Recently he was adjudged as the 'Gourmet Guru' by *Food & Nightlife* magazine. He has been honoured as one of the Top 20 chefs of India.

Vir Sanghvi, the Editorial Director of *Hindustan Times,* said that Kunal is 'the real star of *MasterChef India*.' He has been a judge and a host, along with bollywood actor Akshay Kumar, on India's first reality food show *MasterChef India*. This prestigious show was aired on Star Plus, which is the biggest general entertainment channel in India. He has successfully completed three seasons of *MasterChef India* and is currently a judge and host on *Junior MasterChef India*.

A Note on the Food Stylist

Sujata started as a potter and ended up with her first project as a food stylist with Indranie Dasgupta. Sujata has created some of the most extraordinary food pictures in her career. She has worked on a variety of high-profile food styling assignments, ranging from advertising shoots, restaurant menus, food packaging materials, and consumer products with leading food brands in India. The recipes in this book were created by me but it is her styling that has given the book a breath of life.

A Note on the Photographer

Like with any living being the body is of no use without the soul, the same way the exciting pictures taken by Shirish is the soul of this book. Over the past decade, his work has won numerous awards and recognition, including a silver medal at the prestigious Prix de la Photographie (Paris) in June 2012. His photographs have also been exhibited at the world-renowned Food Photography Festival in Tarragona (Spain) in 2011. His ongoing series, 'American Landscapes', earned an honourable mention at the International Photography Awards (Los Angeles) in 2010. He has an impressive list of prominent advertising and commercial clients.

A Note on the Food Researcher

I met Suyog on the sets of *MasterChef India*, where he was an essential part of the food team for the show. Creative and tireless, Suyog works at creating new flavours and combining cooking techniques to come up with innovative dishes. He is an established food producer in the television world and when he is on a break from the show he is teaching young enthusiasts about food. Suyog and I spent a lot of time researching recipes and scouting the perfect dishes for this book.